The Python Language Reference Manual

for Python version 3.2

Guido van Rossum
Fred L. Drake, Jr., editor

Published by Network Theory Ltd

A catalogue record for this book is available from the British Library.

March 2011 First printing.

This volume supersedes the previous edition for Python 2.5 (ISBN 0954161785)

Published by Network Theory Limited.

Email: info@network-theory.co.uk

ISBN 978-1-906966-14-0

Further information about this book is available from
http://www.network-theory.co.uk/python/language/

This book has an unconditional guarantee. If you are not fully satisfied with your purchase for any reason, please contact the publisher at the address above.

Contents

iv

Publisher's Preface

This manual is part of the official reference documentation for Python, an object-oriented programming language created by Guido van Rossum.

Python is *free software*. The term "free software" refers to your freedom to run, copy, distribute, study, change and improve the software. With Python you have all these freedoms.

You can support free software by becoming an associate member of the Free Software Foundation. The Free Software Foundation is a tax-exempt charity dedicated to promoting the right to use, study, copy, modify, and redistribute computer programs. It also helps to spread awareness of the ethical and political issues of freedom in the use of software. For more information visit the website www.fsf.org.

The development of Python itself is supported by the Python Software Foundation. Companies using Python can invest in the language by becoming sponsoring members of this group. Donations can also be made online through the Python website. Further information is available at http://www.python.org/psf/

Brian Gough
Publisher
March 2011

1. Introduction

This reference manual describes the Python programming language. It is not intended as a tutorial.

While I am trying to be as precise as possible, I chose to use English rather than formal specifications for everything except syntax and lexical analysis. This should make the document more understandable to the average reader, but will leave room for ambiguities. Consequently, if you were coming from Mars and tried to re-implement Python from this document alone, you might have to guess things and in fact you would probably end up implementing quite a different language. On the other hand, if you are using Python and wonder what the precise rules about a particular area of the language are, you should definitely be able to find them here. If you would like to see a more formal definition of the language, maybe you could volunteer your time — or invent a cloning machine :-).

It is dangerous to add too many implementation details to a language reference document — the implementation may change, and other implementations of the same language may work differently. On the other hand, CPython (the original C implementation of Python) is the one Python implementation in widespread use (although alternate implementations continue to gain support), and its particular quirks are sometimes worth being mentioned, especially where the implementation imposes additional limitations. Therefore, you'll find short "implementation notes" sprinkled throughout the text.

Every Python implementation comes with a number of built-in and standard modules. These are documented in *The Python Library Reference Manual*. A few built-in modules are mentioned when they interact in a significant way with the language definition.

1.1. Alternate Implementations

Though there is one Python implementation which is by far the most popular, there are some alternate implementations which are of particular interest to different audiences.

Known implementations include:

CPython This is the original and most-maintained implementation of Python, written in C. New language features generally appear here first.

Jython Python implemented in Java. This implementation can be used as a scripting language for Java applications, or can be used to create applications using the Java class libraries. It is also often used to create tests for Java libraries. More information can be found at the Jython website[1].

Python for .NET This implementation actually uses the CPython implementation, but is a managed .NET application and makes .NET libraries available. It was created by Brian Lloyd. For more information, see the Python for .NET home page[2].

IronPython An alternate Python for .NET. Unlike Python.NET, this is a complete Python implementation that generates IL, and compiles Python code directly to .NET assemblies. It was created by Jim Hugunin, the original creator of Jython. For more information, see the IronPython website[3].

PyPy An implementation of Python written completely in Python. It supports several advanced features not found in other implementations like stackless support and a Just in Time compiler. One of the goals of the project is to encourage experimentation with the language itself by making it easier to modify the interpreter (since it is written in Python). Additional information is available on the PyPy project's home page[4].

Each of these implementations varies in some way from the language as documented in this manual, or introduces specific information beyond what's covered in the standard Python documentation. Please refer to the implementation-specific documentation to determine what else you need to know about the specific implementation you're using.

1.2. Notation

The descriptions of lexical analysis and syntax use a modified BNF grammar notation. This uses the following style of definition:

```
name        ::=   lc_letter (lc_letter | "_")*
lc_letter   ::=   "a"..."z"
```

The first line says that a name is an `lc_letter` followed by a sequence of zero or more `lc_letters` and underscores. An `lc_letter` in turn is any of the single characters 'a' through 'z'. (This rule is actually adhered to for the names defined in lexical and grammar rules in this document.)

Each rule begins with a name (which is the name defined by the rule) and : := . A vertical bar (|) is used to separate alternatives; it is the least binding operator in this notation. A star (*) means zero or more repetitions of the preceding item; likewise, a plus (+) means one or more repetitions, and a phrase enclosed in square brackets ([ ]) means zero or one occurrences (in other words, the enclosed phrase is optional). The * and + operators bind as tightly as possible; parentheses are used for grouping. Literal strings are enclosed in quotes. White space is only meaningful to separate tokens. Rules are normally contained on

---

[1] http://www.jython.org/
[2] http://pythonnet.sourceforge.net
[3] http://www.ironpython.com/
[4] http://pypy.org/

a single line; rules with many alternatives may be formatted alternatively with each line after the first beginning with a vertical bar.

In lexical definitions (as the example above), two more conventions are used: Two literal characters separated by three dots mean a choice of any single character in the given (inclusive) range of ASCII characters. A phrase between angular brackets (<...>) gives an informal description of the symbol defined; e.g., this could be used to describe the notion of 'control character' if needed.

Even though the notation used is almost the same, there is a big difference between the meaning of lexical and syntactic definitions: a lexical definition operates on the individual characters of the input source, while a syntax definition operates on the stream of tokens generated by the lexical analysis. All uses of BNF in the next chapter ("Lexical Analysis") are lexical definitions; uses in subsequent chapters are syntactic definitions.

2. Lexical analysis

A Python program is read by a *parser*. Input to the parser is a stream of *tokens*, generated by the *lexical analyzer*. This chapter describes how the lexical analyzer breaks a file into tokens.

Python reads program text as Unicode code points; the encoding of a source file can be given by an encoding declaration and defaults to UTF-8, see **PEP 3120**[1] for details. If the source file cannot be decoded, a SyntaxError is raised.

2.1. Line structure

A Python program is divided into a number of *logical lines*.

2.1.1. Logical lines

The end of a logical line is represented by the token NEWLINE. Statements cannot cross logical line boundaries except where NEWLINE is allowed by the syntax (e.g., between statements in compound statements). A logical line is constructed from one or more *physical lines* by following the explicit or implicit *line joining* rules.

2.1.2. Physical lines

A physical line is a sequence of characters terminated by an end-of-line sequence. In source files, any of the standard platform line termination sequences can be used - the Unix form using ASCII LF (linefeed), the Windows form using the ASCII sequence CR LF (return followed by linefeed), or the old Macintosh form using the ASCII CR (return) character. All of these forms can be used equally, regardless of platform.

When embedding Python, source code strings should be passed to Python APIs using the standard C conventions for newline characters (the \n character, representing ASCII LF, is the line terminator).

2.1.3. Comments

A comment starts with a hash character (#) that is not part of a string literal, and ends at the end of the physical line. A comment signifies the end of the logical line unless the implicit line joining rules are invoked. Comments are ignored by the syntax; they are not tokens.

---

[1]PEP = "Python Enhancement Proposal", http://www.python.org/dev/peps/pep-3120

2.1.4. Encoding declarations

If a comment in the first or second line of the Python script matches the regular expression coding[=:]\s*([-\w.]+), this comment is processed as an encoding declaration; the first group of this expression names the encoding of the source code file. The recommended forms of this expression are

    # -*- coding: <encoding-name> -*-

which is recognized also by GNU Emacs, and

    # vim:fileencoding=<encoding-name>

which is recognized by Bram Moolenaar's VIM.

If no encoding declaration is found, the default encoding is UTF-8. In addition, if the first bytes of the file are the UTF-8 byte-order mark (b'\xef\xbb\xbf'), the declared file encoding is UTF-8 (this is supported, among others, by Microsoft's **notepad**).

If an encoding is declared, the encoding name must be recognized by Python. The encoding is used for all lexical analysis, including string literals, comments and identifiers. The encoding declaration must appear on a line of its own.

2.1.5. Explicit line joining

Two or more physical lines may be joined into logical lines using backslash characters (\), as follows: when a physical line ends in a backslash that is not part of a string literal or comment, it is joined with the following forming a single logical line, deleting the backslash and the following end-of-line character. For example:

```
if 1900 < year < 2100 and 1 <= month <= 12 \
   and 1 <= day <= 31 and 0 <= hour < 24 \
   and 0 <= minute < 60 and 0 <= second < 60: # Looks like a valid date
      return 1
```

A line ending in a backslash cannot carry a comment. A backslash does not continue a comment. A backslash does not continue a token except for string literals (i.e., tokens other than string literals cannot be split across physical lines using a backslash). A backslash is illegal elsewhere on a line outside a string literal.

2.1.6. Implicit line joining

Expressions in parentheses, square brackets or curly braces can be split over more than one physical line without using backslashes. For example:

```
month_names = [
       'Januari', 'Februari', 'Maart',     # These are the
       'April',   'Mei',      'Juni',      # Dutch names
```

```
'Juli',     'Augustus', 'September',   # for the months
'Oktober', 'November', 'December']   # of the year
```

Implicitly continued lines can carry comments. The indentation of the continuation lines is not important. Blank continuation lines are allowed. There is no NEWLINE token between implicit continuation lines. Implicitly continued lines can also occur within triple-quoted strings (see below); in that case they cannot carry comments.

2.1.7. Blank lines

A logical line that contains only spaces, tabs, formfeeds and possibly a comment, is ignored (i.e., no NEWLINE token is generated). During interactive input of statements, handling of a blank line may differ depending on the implementation of the read-eval-print loop. In the standard interactive interpreter, an entirely blank logical line (i.e. one containing not even whitespace or a comment) terminates a multi-line statement.

2.1.8. Indentation

Leading whitespace (spaces and tabs) at the beginning of a logical line is used to compute the indentation level of the line, which in turn is used to determine the grouping of statements.

Tabs are replaced (from left to right) by one to eight spaces such that the total number of characters up to and including the replacement is a multiple of eight (this is intended to be the same rule as used by Unix). The total number of spaces preceding the first non-blank character then determines the line's indentation. Indentation cannot be split over multiple physical lines using backslashes; the whitespace up to the first backslash determines the indentation.

Indentation is rejected as inconsistent if a source file mixes tabs and spaces in a way that makes the meaning dependent on the worth of a tab in spaces; a TabError is raised in that case.

Cross-platform compatibility note: because of the nature of text editors on non-UNIX platforms, it is unwise to use a mixture of spaces and tabs for the indentation in a single source file. It should also be noted that different platforms may explicitly limit the maximum indentation level.

A formfeed character may be present at the start of the line; it will be ignored for the indentation calculations above. Formfeed characters occurring elsewhere in the leading whitespace have an undefined effect (for instance, they may reset the space count to zero).

The indentation levels of consecutive lines are used to generate INDENT and DEDENT tokens, using a stack, as follows.

Before the first line of the file is read, a single zero is pushed on the stack; this will never be popped off again. The numbers pushed on the stack will always be strictly increasing from bottom to top. At the beginning of each logical line, the line's indentation level is compared to the top of the stack. If it is equal, nothing happens. If it is larger, it is pushed on the stack, and one INDENT token is generated. If it is smaller, it *must* be one of the numbers occurring on the stack; all numbers on the stack that are larger are popped off, and for each number popped off a DEDENT token is generated. At the end of the file, a DEDENT token is generated for each number remaining on the stack that is larger than zero.

Here is an example of a correctly (though confusingly) indented piece of Python code:

```
def perm(l):
            # Compute the list of all permutations of l
    if len(l) <= 1:
                    return [l]
    r = []
    for i in range(len(l)):
            s = l[:i] + l[i+1:]
            p = perm(s)
            for x in p:
             r.append(l[i:i+1] + x)
        return r
```

The following example shows various indentation errors:

```
  def perm(l):                        # error: first line indented
  for i in range(len(l)):             # error: not indented
      s = l[:i] + l[i+1:]
          p = perm(l[:i] + l[i+1:])   # error: unexpected indent
          for x in p:
                  r.append(l[i:i+1] + x)
          return r                    # error: inconsistent dedent
```

(Actually, the first three errors are detected by the parser; only the last error is found by the lexical analyzer — the indentation of return r does not match a level popped off the stack.)

2.1.9. Whitespace between tokens

Except at the beginning of a logical line or in string literals, the whitespace characters space, tab and formfeed can be used interchangeably to separate tokens. Whitespace is needed between two tokens only if their concatenation could otherwise be interpreted as a different token (e.g., ab is one token, but a b is two tokens).

2.2. Other tokens

Besides NEWLINE, INDENT and DEDENT, the following categories of tokens exist: *identifiers*, *keywords*, *literals*, *operators*, and *delimiters*. Whitespace characters (other than line terminators, discussed earlier) are not tokens, but serve to delimit tokens. Where ambiguity exists, a token comprises the longest possible string that forms a legal token, when read from left to right.

2.3. Identifiers and keywords

Identifiers (also referred to as *names*) are described by the following lexical definitions.

The syntax of identifiers in Python is based on the Unicode standard annex UAX-31, with elaboration and changes as defined below; see also **PEP 3131**[2] for further details.

Within the ASCII range (U+0001..U+007F), the valid characters for identifiers are the same as in Python 2.x: the uppercase and lowercase letters A through Z, the underscore _ and, except for the first character, the digits 0 through 9.

Python 3.0 introduces additional characters from outside the ASCII range (see **PEP 3131**). For these characters, the classification uses the version of the Unicode Character Database as included in the unicodedata module.

Identifiers are unlimited in length. Case is significant.

```
identifier   ::=  xid_start xid_continue*
id_start     ::=  <all characters in general categories
                  Lu, Ll, Lt, Lm, Lo, Nl, the underscore,
                  and characters with the Other_ID_Start
                  property>
id_continue  ::=  <all characters in id_start, plus
                  characters in the categories Mn, Mc, Nd,
                  Pc and others with the Other_ID_Continue
                  property>
xid_start    ::=  <all characters in id_start whose
                  NFKC normalization is in "id_start
                  xid_continue*">
xid_continue ::=  <all characters in id_continue whose NFKC
                  normalization is in "id_continue*">
```

The Unicode category codes mentioned above stand for:

- *Lu* - uppercase letters

- *Ll* - lowercase letters

- *Lt* - titlecase letters

- *Lm* - modifier letters

- *Lo* - other letters

- *Nl* - letter numbers

- *Mn* - nonspacing marks

---

[2]http://www.python.org/dev/peps/pep-3131

- *Mc* - spacing combining marks

- *Nd* - decimal numbers

- *Pc* - connector punctuations

- *Other_ ID_ Start* - explicit list of characters in PropList.txt[3] to support backwards compatibility

- *Other_ ID_ Continue* - likewise

All identifiers are converted into the normal form NFKC while parsing; comparison of identifiers is based on NFKC.

A non-normative HTML file listing all valid identifier characters for Unicode 4.1 can be found at http://www.dcl.hpi.uni-potsdam.de/home/loewis/table-3131.html.

2.3.1. Keywords

The following identifiers are used as reserved words, or *keywords* of the language, and cannot be used as ordinary identifiers. They must be spelled exactly as written here:

False	class	finally	is	return
None	continue	for	lambda	try
True	def	from	nonlocal	while
and	del	global	not	with
as	elif	if	or	yield
assert	else	import	pass	
break	except	in	raise	

2.3.2. Reserved classes of identifiers

Certain classes of identifiers (besides keywords) have special meanings. These classes are identified by the patterns of leading and trailing underscore characters:

_* Not imported by from module import *. The special identifier _ is used in the interactive interpreter to store the result of the last evaluation; it is stored in the builtins module. When not in interactive mode, _ has no special meaning and is not defined. See section 6.11 *The import statement* (page 81).

Note: The name _ is often used in conjunction with internationalization; refer to the documentation for the gettext module for more information on this convention.

__*__ System-defined names. These names are defined by the interpreter and its implementation (including the standard library). Current system names are discussed in section 3.3 *Special method names* (page 31) and elsewhere.

---

[3]http://unicode.org/Public/UNIDATA/PropList.txt

More will likely be defined in future versions of Python. *Any* use of __*__ names, in any context, that does not follow explicitly documented use, is subject to breakage without warning.

__* Class-private names. Names in this category, when used within the context of a class definition, are re-written to use a mangled form to help avoid name clashes between "private" attributes of base and derived classes. See section 5.2.1 *Identifiers (Names)* (page 53).

2.4. Literals

Literals are notations for constant values of some built-in types.

2.4.1. String and Bytes literals

String literals are described by the following lexical definitions:

```
stringliteral    ::=  [stringprefix](shortstring |
                      longstring)
stringprefix     ::=  "r" | "R"
shortstring      ::=  "'" shortstringitem* "'" | '"'
                      shortstringitem* '"'
longstring       ::=  "'''" longstringitem* "'''" | '"""'
                      longstringitem* '"""'
shortstringitem  ::=  shortstringchar | stringescapeseq
longstringitem   ::=  longstringchar | stringescapeseq
shortstringchar  ::=  <any source character except "\" or
                      newline or the quote>
longstringchar   ::=  <any source character except "\">
stringescapeseq  ::=  "\" <any source character>

bytesliteral     ::=  bytesprefix(shortbytes | longbytes)
bytesprefix      ::=  "b" | "B" | "br" | "Br" | "bR" | "BR"
shortbytes       ::=  "'" shortbytesitem* "'" | '"'
                      shortbytesitem* '"'
longbytes        ::=  "'''" longbytesitem* "'''" | '"""'
                      longbytesitem* '"""'
shortbytesitem   ::=  shortbyteschar | bytesescapeseq
longbytesitem    ::=  longbyteschar | bytesescapeseq
shortbyteschar   ::=  <any ASCII character except "\" or
                      newline or the quote>
longbyteschar    ::=  <any ASCII character except "\">
bytesescapeseq   ::=  "\" <any ASCII character>
```

One syntactic restriction not indicated by these productions is that whitespace is not allowed between the stringprefix or bytesprefix and the rest of the literal. The source character set is defined by the encoding declaration; it is UTF-8 if no encoding declaration is given in the source file; see section 2.1.4 *Encoding declarations* (page 8).

In plain English: Both types of literals can be enclosed in matching single quotes (') or double quotes ("). They can also be enclosed in matching groups of three single or double quotes (these are generally referred to as *triple-quoted strings*). The backslash (\) character is used to escape characters that otherwise have a special meaning, such as newline, backslash itself, or the quote character.

Bytes literals are always prefixed with 'b' or 'B'; they produce an instance of the bytes type instead of the str type. They may only contain ASCII characters; bytes with a numeric value of 128 or greater must be expressed with escapes.

Both string and bytes literals may optionally be prefixed with a letter 'r' or 'R'; such strings are called *raw strings* and treat backslashes as literal characters. As a result, in string literals, '\U' and '\u' escapes in raw strings are not treated specially.

In triple-quoted strings, unescaped newlines and quotes are allowed (and are retained), except that three unescaped quotes in a row terminate the string. (A "quote" is the character used to open the string, i.e. either ' or ".)

Unless an 'r' or 'R' prefix is present, escape sequences in strings are interpreted according to rules similar to those used by Standard C. The recognized escape sequences are:

Escape Sequence	Meaning	Notes
\newline	Backslash and newline ignored	
\\	Backslash (\)	
\'	Single quote (')	
\"	Double quote (")	
\a	ASCII Bell (BEL)	
\b	ASCII Backspace (BS)	
\f	ASCII Formfeed (FF)	
\n	ASCII Linefeed (LF)	
\r	ASCII Carriage Return (CR)	
\t	ASCII Horizontal Tab (TAB)	
\v	ASCII Vertical Tab (VT)	
\ooo	Character with octal value *ooo*	(1,3)
\xhh	Character with hex value *hh*	(2,3)

Escape sequences only recognized in string literals are:

Escape Sequence	Meaning	Notes
\N{name}	Character named *name* in the Unicode database	
\uxxxx	Character with 16-bit hex value *xxxx*	(4)
\Uxxxxxxxx	Character with 32-bit hex value *xxxxxxxx*	(5)

Notes:

1. As in Standard C, up to three octal digits are accepted.

2. Unlike in Standard C, exactly two hex digits are required.

3. In a bytes literal, hexadecimal and octal escapes denote the byte with the given value. In a string literal, these escapes denote a Unicode character with the given value.

4. Individual code units which form parts of a surrogate pair can be encoded using this escape sequence. Exactly four hex digits are required.

5. Any Unicode character can be encoded this way, but characters outside the Basic Multilingual Plane (BMP) will be encoded using a surrogate pair if Python is compiled to use 16-bit code units (the default). Exactly eight hex digits are required.

Unlike Standard C, all unrecognized escape sequences are left in the string unchanged, i.e., *the backslash is left in the string*. (This behavior is useful when debugging: if an escape sequence is mistyped, the resulting output is more easily recognized as broken.) It is also important to note that the escape sequences only recognized in string literals fall into the category of unrecognized escapes for bytes literals.

Even in a raw string, string quotes can be escaped with a backslash, but the backslash remains in the string; for example, r"\"" is a valid string literal consisting of two characters: a backslash and a double quote; r"\" is not a valid string literal (even a raw string cannot end in an odd number of backslashes). Specifically, *a raw string cannot end in a single backslash* (since the backslash would escape the following quote character). Note also that a single backslash followed by a newline is interpreted as those two characters as part of the string, *not* as a line continuation.

2.4.2. String literal concatenation

Multiple adjacent string or bytes literals (delimited by whitespace), possibly using different quoting conventions, are allowed, and their meaning is the same as their concatenation. Thus, "hello" 'world' is equivalent to "helloworld". This feature can be used to reduce the number of backslashes needed, to split long strings conveniently across long lines, or even to add comments to parts of strings, for example:

```
re.compile("[A-Za-z_]"        # letter or underscore
           "[A-Za-z0-9_]*"    # letter, digit or underscore
          )
```

Note that this feature is defined at the syntactical level, but implemented at compile time. The '+' operator must be used to concatenate string expressions at run time. Also note that literal concatenation can use different quoting styles for each component (even mixing raw strings and triple quoted strings).

2.4.3. Numeric literals

There are three types of numeric literals: integers, floating point numbers, and imaginary numbers. There are no complex literals (complex numbers can be formed by adding a real number and an imaginary number).

Note that numeric literals do not include a sign; a phrase like -1 is actually an expression composed of the unary operator '-' and the literal 1.

2.4.4. Integer literals

Integer literals are described by the following lexical definitions:

```
integer          ::=  decimalinteger | octinteger | hexinteger
                      | bininteger
decimalinteger   ::=  nonzerodigit digit* | "0"+
nonzerodigit     ::=  "1"..."9"
digit            ::=  "0"..."9"
octinteger       ::=  "0" ("o" | "O") octdigit+
hexinteger       ::=  "0" ("x" | "X") hexdigit+
bininteger       ::=  "0" ("b" | "B") bindigit+
octdigit         ::=  "0"..."7"
hexdigit         ::=  digit | "a"..."f" | "A"..."F"
bindigit         ::=  "0" | "1"
```

There is no limit for the length of integer literals apart from what can be stored in available memory.

Note that leading zeros in a non-zero decimal number are not allowed. This is for disambiguation with C-style octal literals, which Python used before version 3.0.

Some examples of integer literals:

```
7    2147483647                           0o177   0b100110111
3    79228162514264337593543950336        0o377   0x100000000
     79228162514264337593543950336                0xdeadbeef
```

2.4.5. Floating point literals

Floating point literals are described by the following lexical definitions:

```
floatnumber      ::=  pointfloat | exponentfloat
pointfloat       ::=  [intpart] fraction | intpart "."
exponentfloat    ::=  (intpart | pointfloat) exponent
intpart          ::=  digit+
fraction         ::=  "." digit+
exponent         ::=  ("e" | "E") ["+" | "-"] digit+
```

Note that the integer and exponent parts are always interpreted using radix 10. For example, 077e010 is legal, and denotes the same number as 77e10.

The allowed range of floating point literals is implementation-dependent. Some examples of floating point literals:

```
3.14    10.    .001    1e100    3.14e-10    0e0
```

Note that numeric literals do not include a sign; a phrase like -1 is actually an expression composed of the unary operator - and the literal 1.

2.4.6. Imaginary literals

Imaginary literals are described by the following lexical definitions:

```
imagnumber  ::=  (floatnumber | intpart) ("j" | "J")
```

An imaginary literal yields a complex number with a real part of 0.0. Complex numbers are represented as a pair of floating point numbers and have the same restrictions on their range. To create a complex number with a nonzero real part, add a floating point number to it, e.g., (3+4j). Some examples of imaginary literals:

```
3.14j    10.j    10j    .001j    1e100j    3.14e-10j
```

2.5. Operators

The following tokens are operators:

```
+       -       *       **      /       //      %
<<      >>      &       |       ^       ~
<       >       <=      >=      ==      !=
```

2.6. Delimiters

The following tokens serve as delimiters in the grammar:

```
(       )       [       ]       {       }
,       :       .       ;       @       =
+=      -=      *=      /=      //=     %=
&=      |=      ^=      >>=     <<=     **=
```

The period can also occur in floating-point and imaginary literals. A sequence of three periods has a special meaning as an ellipsis literal. The second half of the list, the augmented assignment operators, serve lexically as delimiters, but also perform an operation.

The following printing ASCII characters have special meaning as part of other tokens or are otherwise significant to the lexical analyzer:

```
'       "       #       \
```

The following printing ASCII characters are not used in Python. Their occurrence outside string literals and comments is an unconditional error:

```
$       ?       `
```

3. Data model

3.1. Objects, values and types

Objects are Python's abstraction for data. All data in a Python program is represented by objects or by relations between objects. (In a sense, and in conformance to Von Neumann's model of a "stored program computer," code is also represented by objects.)

Every object has an identity, a type and a value. An object's *identity* never changes once it has been created; you may think of it as the object's address in memory. The 'is' operator compares the identity of two objects; the id() function returns an integer representing its identity (currently implemented as its address). An object's *type* is also unchangeable.[1] An object's type determines the operations that the object supports (e.g., "does it have a length?") and also defines the possible values for objects of that type. The type() function returns an object's type (which is an object itself). The *value* of some objects can change. Objects whose value can change are said to be *mutable*; objects whose value is unchangeable once they are created are called *immutable*. (The value of an immutable container object that contains a reference to a mutable object can change when the latter's value is changed; however the container is still considered immutable, because the collection of objects it contains cannot be changed. So, immutability is not strictly the same as having an unchangeable value, it is more subtle.) An object's mutability is determined by its type; for instance, numbers, strings and tuples are immutable, while dictionaries and lists are mutable.

Objects are never explicitly destroyed; however, when they become unreachable they may be garbage-collected. An implementation is allowed to postpone garbage collection or omit it altogether — it is a matter of implementation quality how garbage collection is implemented, as long as no objects are collected that are still reachable.

CPython implementation detail: CPython currently uses a reference-counting scheme with (optional) delayed detection of cyclically linked garbage, which collects most objects as soon as they become unreachable, but is not guaranteed to collect garbage containing circular references. See the documentation of the gc module for information on controlling the collection of cyclic garbage. Other implementations act differently and CPython may change.

Note that the use of the implementation's tracing or debugging facilities may keep objects alive that would normally be collectable. Also note that catching an exception with a 'try...except' statement may keep objects alive.

---

[1] It *is* possible in some cases to change an object's type, under certain controlled conditions. It generally isn't a good idea though, since it can lead to some very strange behaviour if it is handled incorrectly.

Some objects contain references to "external" resources such as open files or windows. It is understood that these resources are freed when the object is garbage-collected, but since garbage collection is not guaranteed to happen, such objects also provide an explicit way to release the external resource, usually a close() method. Programs are strongly recommended to explicitly close such objects. The 'try...finally' statement and the 'with' statement provide convenient ways to do this.

Some objects contain references to other objects; these are called *containers*. Examples of containers are tuples, lists and dictionaries. The references are part of a container's value. In most cases, when we talk about the value of a container, we imply the values, not the identities of the contained objects; however, when we talk about the mutability of a container, only the identities of the immediately contained objects are implied. So, if an immutable container (like a tuple) contains a reference to a mutable object, its value changes if that mutable object is changed.

Types affect almost all aspects of object behavior. Even the importance of object identity is affected in some sense: for immutable types, operations that compute new values may actually return a reference to any existing object with the same type and value, while for mutable objects this is not allowed. E.g., after a = 1; b = 1, a and b may or may not refer to the same object with the value one, depending on the implementation, but after c = []; d = [], c and d are guaranteed to refer to two different, unique, newly created empty lists. (Note that c = d = [] assigns the same object to both c and d.)

3.2. The standard type hierarchy

Below is a list of the types that are built into Python. Extension modules (written in C, Java, or other languages, depending on the implementation) can define additional types. Future versions of Python may add types to the type hierarchy (e.g., rational numbers, efficiently stored arrays of integers, etc.), although such additions will often be provided via the standard library instead.

Some of the type descriptions below contain a paragraph listing 'special attributes.' These are attributes that provide access to the implementation and are not intended for general use. Their definition may change in the future.

None This type has a single value. There is a single object with this value. This object is accessed through the built-in name None. It is used to signify the absence of a value in many situations, e.g., it is returned from functions that don't explicitly return anything. Its truth value is false.

NotImplemented This type has a single value. There is a single object with this value. This object is accessed through the built-in name NotImplemented. Numeric methods and rich comparison methods may return this value if they do not implement the operation for the operands provided. (The interpreter will then try the reflected operation, or some other fallback, depending on the operator.) Its truth value is true.

Ellipsis This type has a single value. There is a single object with this value. This object is accessed through the literal ... or the built-in name Ellipsis. Its truth value is true.

numbers.Number These are created by numeric literals and returned as results by arithmetic operators and arithmetic built-in functions. Numeric objects are immutable; once created their value never changes. Python numbers are of course strongly related to mathematical numbers, but subject to the limitations of numerical representation in computers.

Python distinguishes between integers, floating point numbers, and complex numbers:

numbers.Integral These represent elements from the mathematical set of integers (positive and negative).

There are two types of integers:

Integers (int) These represent numbers in an unlimited range, subject to available (virtual) memory only. For the purpose of shift and mask operations, a binary representation is assumed, and negative numbers are represented in a variant of 2's complement which gives the illusion of an infinite string of sign bits extending to the left.

Booleans (bool) These represent the truth values False and True. The two objects representing the values False and True are the only Boolean objects. The Boolean type is a subtype of the integer type, and Boolean values behave like the values 0 and 1, respectively, in almost all contexts, the exception being that when converted to a string, the strings "False" or "True" are returned, respectively.

The rules for integer representation are intended to give the most meaningful interpretation of shift and mask operations involving negative integers.

numbers.Real (float) These represent machine-level double precision floating point numbers. You are at the mercy of the underlying machine architecture (and C or Java implementation) for the accepted range and handling of overflow. Python does not support single-precision floating point numbers; the savings in processor and memory usage that are usually the reason for using these is dwarfed by the overhead of using objects in Python, so there is no reason to complicate the language with two kinds of floating point numbers.

numbers.Complex (complex) These represent complex numbers as a pair of machine-level double precision floating point numbers. The same caveats apply as for floating point numbers. The real and imaginary parts of a complex number z can be retrieved through the read-only attributes z.real and z.imag.

Sequences These represent finite ordered sets indexed by non-negative numbers. The built-in function len() returns the number of items of a sequence.

When the length of a sequence is n, the index set contains the numbers 0, 1, ..., n-1. Item i of sequence a is selected by a[i].

Sequences also support slicing: a[i:j] selects all items with index k such that $i <= k < j$. When used as an expression, a slice is a sequence of the same type. This implies that the index set is renumbered so that it starts at 0.

Some sequences also support "extended slicing" with a third "step" parameter: a[i:j:k] selects all items of a with index x where x = i + n*k, n >= 0 and $i <= x < j$.

Sequences are distinguished according to their mutability:

Immutable sequences An object of an immutable sequence type cannot change once it is created. (If the object contains references to other objects, these other objects may be mutable and may be changed; however, the collection of objects directly referenced by an immutable object cannot change.)

The following types are immutable sequences:

Strings The items of a string object are Unicode code units. A Unicode code unit is represented by a string object of one item and can hold either a 16-bit or 32-bit value representing a Unicode ordinal (the maximum value for the ordinal is given in sys.maxunicode, and depends on how Python is configured at compile time). Surrogate pairs may be present in the Unicode object, and will be reported as two separate items. The built-in functions chr() and ord() convert between code units and nonnegative integers representing the Unicode ordinals as defined in the Unicode Standard 3.0. Conversion from and to other encodings are possible through the string method encode().

Tuples The items of a tuple are arbitrary Python objects. Tuples of two or more items are formed by comma-separated lists of expressions. A tuple of one item (a 'singleton') can be formed by affixing a comma to an expression (an expression by itself does not create a tuple, since parentheses must be usable for grouping of expressions). An empty tuple can be formed by an empty pair of parentheses.

Bytes A bytes object is an immutable array. The items are 8-bit bytes, represented by integers in the range $0 <= x < 256$. Bytes literals (like b'abc' and the built-in function bytes() can be used to construct bytes objects. Also, bytes objects can be decoded to strings via the decode() method.

Mutable sequences Mutable sequences can be changed after they are created. The subscription and slicing notations can be used as the target of assignment and del (delete) statements.

There are currently two intrinsic mutable sequence types:

Lists The items of a list are arbitrary Python objects. Lists are formed by placing a comma-separated list of expressions in square brackets. (Note that there are no special cases needed to form lists of length 0 or 1.)

Byte Arrays A bytearray object is a mutable array. They are created by the built-in `bytearray()` constructor. Aside from being mutable (and hence unhashable), byte arrays otherwise provide the same interface and functionality as immutable bytes objects.

The extension module `array` provides an additional example of a mutable sequence type, as does the `collections` module.

Set types These represent unordered, finite sets of unique, immutable objects. As such, they cannot be indexed by any subscript. However, they can be iterated over, and the built-in function `len()` returns the number of items in a set. Common uses for sets are fast membership testing, removing duplicates from a sequence, and computing mathematical operations such as intersection, union, difference, and symmetric difference.

For set elements, the same immutability rules apply as for dictionary keys. Note that numeric types obey the normal rules for numeric comparison: if two numbers compare equal (e.g., 1 and 1.0), only one of them can be contained in a set.

There are currently two intrinsic set types:

Sets These represent a mutable set. They are created by the built-in `set()` constructor and can be modified afterwards by several methods, such as `add()`.

Frozen sets These represent an immutable set. They are created by the built-in `frozenset()` constructor. As a frozenset is immutable and *hashable*, it can be used again as an element of another set, or as a dictionary key.

Mappings These represent finite sets of objects indexed by arbitrary index sets. The subscript notation a[k] selects the item indexed by k from the mapping a; this can be used in expressions and as the target of assignments or del statements. The built-in function `len()` returns the number of items in a mapping.

There is currently a single intrinsic mapping type:

Dictionaries These represent finite sets of objects indexed by nearly arbitrary values. The only types of values not acceptable as keys are values containing lists or dictionaries or other mutable types that are compared by value rather than by object identity, the reason being that the efficient implementation of dictionaries requires a key's hash value to remain constant. Numeric types used for keys obey the normal rules for numeric comparison: if two numbers compare equal (e.g., 1 and 1.0) then they can be used interchangeably to index the same dictionary entry.

Dictionaries are mutable; they can be created by the {...} notation (see section 5.2.7 *Dictionary displays*, page 56).

The extension modules dbm.ndbm and dbm.gnu provide additional examples of mapping types, as does the collections module.

Callable types These are the types to which the function call operation (see section 5.3.4 *Calls*, page 61) can be applied:

User-defined functions A user-defined function object is created by a function definition (see section 7.6 *Function definitions*, page 94). It should be called with an argument list containing the same number of items as the function's formal parameter list.

Special attributes:

Attribute	Meaning	
__doc__	The function's documentation string, or None if unavailable	Writable
__name__	The function's name	Writable
__module__	The name of the module the function was defined in, or None if unavailable.	Writable
__defaults__	A tuple containing default argument values for those arguments that have defaults, or None if no arguments have a default value	Writable
__code__	The code object representing the compiled function body.	Writable
__globals__	A reference to the dictionary that holds the function's global variables — the global namespace of the module in which the function was defined.	Read-only
__dict__	The namespace supporting arbitrary function attributes.	Writable
__closure__	None or a tuple of cells that contain bindings for the function's free variables.	Read-only
__annotations__	A dict containing annotations of parameters. The keys of the dict are the parameter names, or 'return' for the return annotation, if provided.	Writable
__kwdefaults__	A dict containing defaults for keyword-only parameters.	Writable

Most of the attributes labelled "Writable" check the type of the assigned value.

Function objects also support getting and setting arbitrary attributes, which can be used, for example, to attach metadata to functions. Regular attribute dot-notation is used to get and set such attributes. *Note that the current implementation only supports function attributes on user-defined functions. Function attributes on built-in functions may be supported in the future.*

Additional information about a function's definition can be retrieved from its code object; see the description of internal types below.

Instance methods An instance method object combines a class, a class instance and any callable object (normally a user-defined function).

Special read-only attributes: __self__ is the class instance object, __func__ is the function object; __doc__ is the method's documentation (same as __func__.__doc__); __name__ is the method name (same as __func__.__name__); __module__ is the name of the module the method was defined in, or None if unavailable.

Methods also support accessing (but not setting) the arbitrary function attributes on the underlying function object.

User-defined method objects may be created when getting an attribute of a class (perhaps via an instance of that class), if that attribute is a user-defined function object or a class method object.

When an instance method object is created by retrieving a user-defined function object from a class via one of its instances, its __self__ attribute is the instance, and the method object is said to be bound. The new method's __func__ attribute is the original function object.

When a user-defined method object is created by retrieving another method object from a class or instance, the behaviour is the same as for a function object, except that the __func__ attribute of the new instance is not the original method object but its __func__ attribute.

When an instance method object is created by retrieving a class method object from a class or instance, its __self__ attribute is the class itself, and its __func__ attribute is the function object underlying the class method.

When an instance method object is called, the underlying function (__func__) is called, inserting the class instance (__self__) in front of the argument list. For instance, when C is a class which contains a definition for a function f(), and x is an instance of C, calling x.f(1) is equivalent to calling C.f(x, 1).

When an instance method object is derived from a class method object, the "class instance" stored in __self__ will actually be the class itself, so that calling either x.f(1) or C.f(1) is equivalent to calling f(C,1) where f is the underlying function.

Note that the transformation from function object to instance method object happens each time the attribute is retrieved from the instance. In some cases, a fruitful optimization is to assign the attribute to a local variable and call that local variable. Also notice that this transformation only happens for user-defined functions; other callable objects (and all non-callable objects) are retrieved without transformation. It is also important to note that user-defined functions which are attributes of a class instance are not converted to bound methods; this *only* happens when the function is an attribute of the class.

Generator functions A function or method which uses the yield statement (see section 6.7 *The yield statement*, page 79) is called a *generator function*. Such a function, when called, always returns an iterator object which can be used to execute the body of the function: calling the iterator's __next__() method will cause the function to execute until it provides a value using the yield statement. When the function executes a return statement or falls off the end, a StopIteration exception is raised and the iterator will have reached the end of the set of values to be returned.

Built-in functions A built-in function object is a wrapper around a C function. Examples of built-in functions are len() and math.sin() (math is a standard built-in module). The number and type of the arguments are determined by the C function. Special read-only attributes: __doc__ is the function's documentation string, or None if unavailable; __name__ is the function's name; __self__ is set to None (but see the next item); __module__ is the name of the module the function was defined in or None if unavailable.

Built-in methods This is really a different disguise of a built-in function, this time containing an object passed to the C function as an implicit extra argument. An example of a built-in method is alist.append(), assuming *alist* is a list object. In this case, the special read-only attribute __self__ is set to the object denoted by *alist*.

Classes Classes are callable. These objects normally act as factories for new instances of themselves, but variations are possible for class types that override __new__(). The arguments of the call are passed to __new__() and, in the typical case, to __init__() to initialize the new instance.

Class Instances Instances of arbitrary classes can be made callable by defining a __call__() method in their class.

Modules Modules are imported by the import statement (see section 6.11 *The import statement*, page 81). A module object has a namespace implemented by a dictionary object (this is the dictionary referenced by the __globals__ attribute of functions defined in the module). Attribute references are translated to lookups in this dictionary, e.g., m.x is equivalent to m.__dict__["x"]. A module object does not contain the code object used to initialize the module (since it isn't needed once the initialization is done).

Attribute assignment updates the module's namespace dictionary, e.g., m.x = 1 is equivalent to m.__dict__["x"] = 1.

Special read-only attribute: __dict__ is the module's namespace as a dictionary object.

CPython implementation detail: Because of the way CPython clears module dictionaries, the module dictionary will be cleared when the module falls out of scope even if the dictionary still has live references. To avoid this, copy the dictionary or keep the module around while using its dictionary directly.

Predefined (writable) attributes: __name__ is the module's name; __doc__ is the module's documentation string, or None if unavailable; __file__ is the pathname of the file from which the module was loaded, if it was loaded from a file. The __file__ attribute is not present for C modules that are statically linked into the interpreter; for extension modules loaded dynamically from a shared library, it is the pathname of the shared library file.

Custom classes Custom class types are typically created by class definitions (see section 7.7 *Class definitions*, page 97). A class has a namespace implemented by a dictionary object. Class attribute references are translated to lookups in this dictionary, e.g., C.x is translated to C.__dict__["x"] (although there are a number of hooks which allow for other means of locating attributes). When the attribute name is not found there, the attribute search continues in the base classes. This search of the base classes uses the C3 method resolution order which behaves correctly even in the presence of 'diamond' inheritance structures where there are multiple inheritance paths leading back to a common ancestor. Additional details on the C3 MRO used by Python can be found in the documentation accompanying the 2.3 release at http://www.python.org/download/releases/2.3/mro/.

When a class attribute reference (for class C, say) would yield a class method object, it is transformed into an instance method object whose __self__ attributes is C. When it would yield a static method object, it is transformed into the object wrapped by the static method object. See section 3.3.2 *Implementing Descriptors* (page 36) for another way in which attributes retrieved from a class may differ from those actually contained in its __dict__.

Class attribute assignments update the class's dictionary, never the dictionary of a base class.

A class object can be called (see above) to yield a class instance (see below).

Special attributes: __name__ is the class name; __module__ is the module name in which the class was defined; __dict__ is the dictionary containing the class's namespace; __bases__ is a tuple (possibly empty or a singleton) containing the base classes, in the order of their occurrence in the base class list; `__doc__` is the class's documentation string, or None if undefined.

Class instances A class instance is created by calling a class object (see above). A class instance has a namespace implemented as a dictionary which is the first place in which attribute references are searched. When an attribute is not found there, and the instance's class has an attribute by that name, the search continues with the class attributes. If a class attribute is found that is a user-defined function object, it is transformed into an instance method object whose `__self__` attribute is the instance. Static method and class method objects are also transformed; see above under "Classes". See section 3.3.2 *Implementing Descriptors* (page 36) for another way in which attributes of a class retrieved via its instances may differ from the objects actually stored in the class's `__dict__`. If no class attribute is found, and the object's class has a `__getattr__()` method, that is called to satisfy the lookup.

Attribute assignments and deletions update the instance's dictionary, never a class's dictionary. If the class has a `__setattr__()` or `__delattr__()` method, this is called instead of updating the instance dictionary directly.

Class instances can pretend to be numbers, sequences, or mappings if they have methods with certain special names. See section 3.3 *Special method names* (page 31).

Special attributes: `__dict__` is the attribute dictionary; `__class__` is the instance's class.

I/O objects (also known as file objects) A *file object* represents an open file. Various shortcuts are available to create file objects: the open() built-in function, and also os.popen(), os.fdopen(), and the makefile() method of socket objects (and perhaps by other functions or methods provided by extension modules).

The objects sys.stdin, sys.stdout and sys.stderr are initialized to file objects corresponding to the interpreter's standard input, output and error streams; they are all open in text mode and therefore follow the interface defined by the io.TextIOBase abstract class.

Internal types A few types used internally by the interpreter are exposed to the user. Their definitions may change with future versions of the interpreter, but they are mentioned here for completeness.

Code objects Code objects represent *byte-compiled* executable Python code, or *bytecode*. The difference between a code object and a function object is that the function object contains an explicit reference to the function's globals (the module in which it was defined), while a code object contains no context; also the default argument values are stored in the function object, not in the code object (because they represent values calculated at run-time). Unlike function objects, code objects are immutable and contain no references (directly or indirectly) to mutable objects.

Special read-only attributes: `co_name` gives the function name; `co_argcount` is the number of positional arguments (including arguments with default values); `co_nlocals` is the number of local variables used by the function (including arguments); `co_varnames` is a tuple containing the names of the local variables (starting with the argument names); `co_cellvars` is a tuple containing the names of local variables that are referenced by nested functions; `co_freevars` is a tuple containing the names of free variables; `co_code` is a string representing the sequence of bytecode instructions; `co_consts` is a tuple containing the literals used by the bytecode; `co_names` is a tuple containing the names used by the bytecode; `co_filename` is the filename from which the code was compiled; `co_firstlineno` is the first line number of the function; `co_lnotab` is a string encoding the mapping from bytecode offsets to line numbers (for details see the source code of the interpreter); `co_stacksize` is the required stack size (including local variables); `co_flags` is an integer encoding a number of flags for the interpreter.

The following flag bits are defined for `co_flags`: bit 0x04 is set if the function uses the *arguments syntax to accept an arbitrary number of positional arguments; bit 0x08 is set if the function uses the **keywords syntax to accept arbitrary keyword arguments; bit 0x20 is set if the function is a generator.

Future feature declarations (from `__future__` import division) also use bits in `co_flags` to indicate whether a code object was compiled with a particular feature enabled: bit 0x2000 is set if the function was compiled with future division enabled; bits 0x10 and 0x1000 were used in earlier versions of Python.

Other bits in `co_flags` are reserved for internal use.

If a code object represents a function, the first item in `co_consts` is the documentation string of the function, or None if undefined.

Frame objects Frame objects represent execution frames. They may occur in traceback objects (see below).

Special read-only attributes: `f_back` is to the previous stack frame (towards the caller), or None if this is the bottom stack frame; `f_code` is the code object being executed in this frame; `f_locals` is the dictionary used to look up local variables; `f_globals` is used for global variables; `f_builtins` is used for built-in (intrinsic) names; `f_lasti` gives the precise instruction (this is an index into the bytecode string of the code object).

Special writable attributes: `f_trace`, if not None, is a function called at the start of each source code line (this is used by the debugger); `f_lineno` is the current line number of the frame — writing to this from within a trace function jumps to the given line (only for the bottom-most frame). A debugger can implement a Jump command (aka Set Next Statement) by writing to f_lineno.

Traceback objects Traceback objects represent a stack trace of an exception. A traceback object is created when an exception occurs. When the search for an exception handler unwinds the execution stack, at each unwound level a traceback object is inserted in front of the current traceback. When an exception handler is entered, the stack trace is made available to the program. (See section 7.4 *The try statement*, page 91.) It is accessible as the third item of the tuple returned by sys.exc_info(). When the program contains no suitable handler, the stack trace is written (nicely formatted) to the standard error stream; if the interpreter is interactive, it is also made available to the user as sys.last_traceback.

Special read-only attributes: tb_next is the next level in the stack trace (towards the frame where the exception occurred), or None if there is no next level; tb_frame points to the execution frame of the current level; tb_lineno gives the line number where the exception occurred; tb_lasti indicates the precise instruction. The line number and last instruction in the traceback may differ from the line number of its frame object if the exception occurred in a try statement with no matching except clause or with a finally clause.

Slice objects Slice objects are used to represent slices for __getitem__() methods. They are also created by the built-in slice() function.

Special read-only attributes: start is the lower bound; stop is the upper bound; step is the step value; each is None if omitted. These attributes can have any type.

Slice objects support one method:

slice.indices(*self, length*)
    This method takes a single integer argument *length* and computes information about the slice that the slice object would describe if applied to a sequence of *length* items. It returns a tuple of three integers; respectively these are the *start* and *stop* indices and the *step* or stride length of the slice. Missing or out-of-bounds indices are handled in a manner consistent with regular slices.

Static method objects Static method objects provide a way of defeating the transformation of function objects to method objects described above. A static method object is a wrapper around any other object, usually a user-defined method object. When a static method object is retrieved from a class or a class instance, the object actually returned is the wrapped object, which is not subject to any further transformation. Static method objects are not themselves callable, although the objects they wrap usually are. Static method objects are created by the built-in `staticmethod()` constructor.

Class method objects A class method object, like a static method object, is a wrapper around another object that alters the way in which that object is retrieved from classes and class instances. The behaviour of class method objects upon such retrieval is described above, under "User-defined methods". Class method objects are created by the built-in `classmethod()` constructor.

3.3. Special method names

A class can implement certain operations that are invoked by special syntax (such as arithmetic operations or subscripting and slicing) by defining methods with special names. This is Python's approach to *operator overloading*, allowing classes to define their own behavior with respect to language operators. For instance, if a class defines a method named `__getitem__()`, and x is an instance of this class, then x[i] is roughly equivalent to `type(x).__getitem__(x, i)`. Except where mentioned, attempts to execute an operation raise an exception when no appropriate method is defined (typically `AttributeError` or `TypeError`).

When implementing a class that emulates any built-in type, it is important that the emulation only be implemented to the degree that it makes sense for the object being modelled. For example, some sequences may work well with retrieval of individual elements, but extracting a slice may not make sense. (One example of this is the `NodeList` interface in the W3C's Document Object Model.)

3.3.1. Basic customization

`object.__new__(cls[, ...])`
Called to create a new instance of class *cls*. `__new__()` is a static method (special-cased so you need not declare it as such) that takes the class of which an instance was requested as its first argument. The remaining arguments are those passed to the object constructor expression (the call to the class). The return value of `__new__()` should be the new object instance (usually an instance of *cls*).

Typical implementations create a new instance of the class by invoking the superclass's `__new__()` method using `super(currentclass, cls).__new__(cls[, ...])` with appropriate arguments and then modifying the newly-created instance as necessary before returning it.

If `__new__()` returns an instance of *cls*, then the new instance's `__init__()` method will be invoked like `__init__(self[, ...])`, where *self* is the new instance and the remaining arguments are the same as were passed to `__new__()`.

If `__new__()` does not return an instance of *cls*, then the new instance's `__init__()` method will not be invoked.

__new__() is intended mainly to allow subclasses of immutable types (like int, str, or tuple) to customize instance creation. It is also commonly overridden in custom metaclasses in order to customize class creation.

object.__init__(*self*[, ...])

Called when the instance is created. The arguments are those passed to the class constructor expression. If a base class has an __init__() method, the derived class's __init__() method, if any, must explicitly call it to ensure proper initialization of the base class part of the instance; for example: BaseClass.__init__(self, [args...]). As a special constraint on constructors, no value may be returned; doing so will cause a TypeError to be raised at runtime.

object.__del__(*self*)

Called when the instance is about to be destroyed. This is also called a destructor. If a base class has a __del__() method, the derived class's __del__() method, if any, must explicitly call it to ensure proper deletion of the base class part of the instance. Note that it is possible (though not recommended!) for the __del__() method to postpone destruction of the instance by creating a new reference to it. It may then be called at a later time when this new reference is deleted. It is not guaranteed that __del__() methods are called for objects that still exist when the interpreter exits.

Note: del x doesn't directly call x.__del__() — the former decrements the reference count for x by one, and the latter is only called when x's reference count reaches zero. Some common situations that may prevent the reference count of an object from going to zero include: circular references between objects (e.g., a doubly-linked list or a tree data structure with parent and child pointers); a reference to the object on the stack frame of a function that caught an exception (the traceback stored in sys.exc_info()[2] keeps the stack frame alive); or a reference to the object on the stack frame that raised an unhandled exception in interactive mode (the traceback stored in sys.last_traceback keeps the stack frame alive). The first situation can only be remedied by explicitly breaking the cycles; the latter two situations can be resolved by storing None in sys.last_traceback. Circular references which are garbage are detected when the option cycle detector is enabled (it's on by default), but can only be cleaned up if there are no Python- level __del__() methods involved. Refer to the documentation for the gc module for more information about how __del__() methods are handled by the cycle detector, particularly the description of the garbage value.

> **Warning:** Due to the precarious circumstances under which `__del__()` methods are invoked, exceptions that occur during their execution are ignored, and a warning is printed to `sys.stderr` instead. Also, when `__del__()` is invoked in response to a module being deleted (e.g., when execution of the program is done), other globals referenced by the `__del__()` method may already have been deleted or in the process of being torn down (e.g. the import machinery shutting down). For this reason, `__del__()` methods should do the absolute minimum needed to maintain external invariants. Starting with version 1.5, Python guarantees that globals whose name begins with a single underscore are deleted from their module before other globals are deleted; if no other references to such globals exist, this may help in assuring that imported modules are still available at the time when the `__del__()` method is called.

object.`__repr__`(*self*)

Called by the `repr()` built-in function to compute the "official" string representation of an object. If at all possible, this should look like a valid Python expression that could be used to recreate an object with the same value (given an appropriate environment). If this is not possible, a string of the form `<...some useful description...>` should be returned. The return value must be a string object. If a class defines `__repr__()` but not `__str__()`, then `__repr__()` is also used when an "informal" string representation of instances of that class is required.

This is typically used for debugging, so it is important that the representation is information-rich and unambiguous.

object.`__str__`(*self*)

Called by the `str()` built-in function and by the `print()` function to compute the "informal" string representation of an object. This differs from `__repr__()` in that it does not have to be a valid Python expression: a more convenient or concise representation may be used instead. The return value must be a string object.

object.`__format__`(*self, format_spec*)

Called by the `format()` built-in function (and by extension, the `format()` method of class `str`) to produce a "formatted" string representation of an object. The `format_spec` argument is a string that contains a description of the formatting options desired. The interpretation of the `format_spec` argument is up to the type implementing `__format__()`, however most classes will either delegate formatting to one of the built-in types, or use a similar formatting option syntax.

See *Format Specification Mini-Language* in "The Python Library Reference Manual" for a description of the standard formatting syntax.

The return value must be a string object.

object.`__lt__`(*self, other*)

```
object.__le__(self, other)
object.__eq__(self, other)
object.__ne__(self, other)
object.__gt__(self, other)
object.__ge__(self, other)
```

These are the so-called "rich comparison" methods. The correspondence between operator symbols and method names is as follows: x<y calls x.__lt__(y), x<=y calls x.__le__(y), x==y calls x.__eq__(y), x!=y calls x.__ne__(y), x>y calls x.__gt__(y), and x>=y calls x.__ge__(y).

A rich comparison method may return the singleton NotImplemented if it does not implement the operation for a given pair of arguments. By convention, False and True are returned for a successful comparison. However, these methods can return any value, so if the comparison operator is used in a Boolean context (e.g., in the condition of an if statement), Python will call bool() on the value to determine if the result is true or false.

There are no implied relationships among the comparison operators. The truth of x==y does not imply that x!=y is false. Accordingly, when defining __eq__(), one should also define __ne__() so that the operators will behave as expected. See the paragraph on __hash__() for some important notes on creating *hashable* objects which support custom comparison operations and are usable as dictionary keys.

There are no swapped-argument versions of these methods (to be used when the left argument does not support the operation but the right argument does); rather, __lt__() and __gt__() are each other's reflection, __le__() and __ge__() are each other's reflection, and __eq__() and __ne__() are their own reflection.

Arguments to rich comparison methods are never coerced.

To automatically generate ordering operations from a single root operation, see functools.total_ordering().

```
object.__hash__(self)
```

Called by built-in function hash() and for operations on members of hashed collections including set, frozenset, and dict. __hash__() should return an integer. The only required property is that objects which compare equal have the same hash value; it is advised to somehow mix together (e.g. using exclusive or) the hash values for the components of the object that also play a part in comparison of objects.

If a class does not define an __eq__() method it should not define a __hash__() operation either; if it defines __eq__() but not __hash__(), its instances will not be usable as items in hashable collections. If a class defines mutable objects and implements an __eq__() method, it should not implement __hash__(), since the implementation of hashable collections requires that a key's hash value is immutable (if the object's hash value changes, it will be in the wrong hash bucket).

User-defined classes have __eq__() and __hash__() methods by default; with them, all objects compare unequal (except with themselves) and x.__hash__() returns id(x).

Classes which inherit a __hash__() method from a parent class but change the meaning of __eq__() such that the hash value returned is no longer appropriate (e.g. by switching to a value-based concept of equality instead of the default identity based equality) can explicitly flag themselves as being unhashable by setting __hash__ = None in the class definition. Doing so means that not only will instances of the class raise an appropriate TypeError when a program attempts to retrieve their hash value, but they will also be correctly identified as unhashable when checking isinstance(obj, collections.Hashable) (unlike classes which define their own __hash__() to explicitly raise TypeError).

If a class that overrides __eq__() needs to retain the implementation of __hash__() from a parent class, the interpreter must be told this explicitly by setting __hash__ = <ParentClass>.__hash__. Otherwise the inheritance of __hash__() will be blocked, just as if __hash__ had been explicitly set to None.

object.__bool__(*self*)
>   Called to implement truth value testing and the built-in operation bool(); should return False or True. When this method is not defined, __len__() is called, if it is defined, and the object is considered true if its result is nonzero. If a class defines neither __len__() nor __bool__(), all its instances are considered true.

3.3.2. Customizing attribute access

The following methods can be defined to customize the meaning of attribute access (use of, assignment to, or deletion of x.name) for class instances.

object.__getattr__(*self, name*)
>   Called when an attribute lookup has not found the attribute in the usual places (i.e. it is not an instance attribute nor is it found in the class tree for self). name is the attribute name. This method should return the (computed) attribute value or raise an AttributeError exception.

>   Note that if the attribute is found through the normal mechanism, __getattr__() is not called. (This is an intentional asymmetry between __getattr__() and __setattr__().) This is done both for efficiency reasons and because otherwise __getattr__() would have no way to access other attributes of the instance. Note that at least for instance variables, you can fake total control by not inserting any values in the instance attribute dictionary (but instead inserting them in another object). See the __getattribute__() method below for a way to actually get total control over attribute access.

`object.__getattribute__(`*self, name*`)`
  Called unconditionally to implement attribute accesses for instances of
  the class. If the class also defines `__getattr__()`, the latter will not
  be called unless `__getattribute__()` either calls it explicitly or raises an
  `AttributeError`. This method should return the (computed) attribute value
  or raise an `AttributeError` exception. In order to avoid infinite recur-
  sion in this method, its implementation should always call the base class
  method with the same name to access any attributes it needs, for example,
  `object.__getattribute__(self, name)`.

  Note: This method may still be bypassed when looking up special methods
  as the result of implicit invocation via language syntax or built-in functions.
  See 3.3.9 *Special method lookup* (page 46).

`object.__setattr__(`*self, name, value*`)`
  Called when an attribute assignment is attempted. This is called instead of
  the normal mechanism (i.e. store the value in the instance dictionary). *name*
  is the attribute name, *value* is the value to be assigned to it.

  If `__setattr__()` wants to assign to an instance attribute, it should
  call the base class method with the same name, for example,
  `object.__setattr__(self, name, value)`.

`object.__delattr__(`*self, name*`)`
  Like `__setattr__()` but for attribute deletion instead of assignment. This
  should only be implemented if `del obj.name` is meaningful for the object.

`object.__dir__(`*self*`)`
  Called when `dir()` is called on the object. A list must be returned.

Implementing Descriptors

The following methods only apply when an instance of the class containing the
method (a so-called *descriptor* class) appears in the class dictionary of another
class, known as the *owner* class. In the examples below, "the attribute" refers
to the attribute whose name is the key of the property in the owner class'
`__dict__`.

`object.__get__(`*self, instance, owner*`)`
  Called to get the attribute of the owner class (class attribute access) or of an
  instance of that class (instance attribute access). *owner* is always the owner
  class, while *instance* is the instance that the attribute was accessed through,
  or `None` when the attribute is accessed through the *owner*. This method
  should return the (computed) attribute value or raise an `AttributeError`
  exception.

`object.__set__(`*self, instance, value*`)`
  Called to set the attribute on an instance *instance* of the owner class to a
  new value, *value*.

`object.__delete__(`*self, instance*`)`
Called to delete the attribute on an instance *instance* of the owner class.

Invoking Descriptors

In general, a descriptor is an object attribute with "binding behavior", one whose attribute access has been overridden by methods in the descriptor protocol: `__get__()`, `__set__()`, and `__delete__()`. If any of those methods are defined for an object, it is said to be a descriptor.

The default behavior for attribute access is to get, set, or delete the attribute from an object's dictionary. For instance, `a.x` has a lookup chain starting with `a.__dict__['x']`, then `type(a).__dict__['x']`, and continuing through the base classes of `type(a)` excluding metaclasses.

However, if the looked-up value is an object defining one of the descriptor methods, then Python may override the default behavior and invoke the descriptor method instead. Where this occurs in the precedence chain depends on which descriptor methods were defined and how they were called.

The starting point for descriptor invocation is a binding, `a.x`. How the arguments are assembled depends on a:

Direct Call The simplest and least common call is when user code directly invokes a descriptor method: `x.__get__(a)`.

Instance Binding If binding to an object instance, `a.x` is transformed into the call: `type(a).__dict__['x'].__get__(a, type(a))`.

Class Binding If binding to a class, `A.x` is transformed into the call: `A.__dict__['x'].__get__(None, A)`.

Super Binding If a is an instance of super, then the binding `super(B, obj).m()` searches `obj.__class__.__mro__` for the base class A immediately preceding B and then invokes the descriptor with the call: `A.__dict__['m'].__get__(obj, A)`.

For instance bindings, the precedence of descriptor invocation depends on the which descriptor methods are defined. A descriptor can define any combination of `__get__()`, `__set__()` and `__delete__()`. If it does not define `__get__()`, then accessing the attribute will return the descriptor object itself unless there is a value in the object's instance dictionary. If the descriptor defines `__set__()` and/or `__delete__()`, it is a data descriptor; if it defines neither, it is a non-data descriptor. Normally, data descriptors define both `__get__()` and `__set__()`, while non-data descriptors have just the `__get__()` method. Data descriptors with `__set__()` and `__get__()` defined always override a redefinition in an instance dictionary. In contrast, non-data descriptors can be overridden by instances.

Python methods (including `staticmethod()` and `classmethod()`) are implemented as non-data descriptors. Accordingly, instances can redefine and override methods. This allows individual instances to acquire behaviors that differ from other instances of the same class.

The property() function is implemented as a data descriptor. Accordingly, instances cannot override the behavior of a property.

_ _ slots _ _

By default, instances of classes have a dictionary for attribute storage. This wastes space for objects having very few instance variables. The space consumption can become acute when creating large numbers of instances.

The default can be overridden by defining _ _ slots _ _ in a class definition. The _ _ slots _ _ declaration takes a sequence of instance variables and reserves just enough space in each instance to hold a value for each variable. Space is saved because _ _ dict _ _ is not created for each instance.

object.__slots__
   This class variable can be assigned a string, iterable, or sequence of strings with variable names used by instances. If defined in a class, _ _ slots _ _ reserves space for the declared variables and prevents the automatic creation of _ _ dict _ _ and _ _ weakref _ _ for each instance.

Notes on using _ _ slots _ _

- When inheriting from a class without _ _ slots _ _ , the _ _ dict _ _ attribute of that class will always be accessible, so a _ _ slots _ _ definition in the subclass is meaningless.

- Without a _ _ dict _ _ variable, instances cannot be assigned new variables not listed in the _ _ slots _ _ definition. Attempts to assign to an unlisted variable name raises AttributeError. If dynamic assignment of new variables is desired, then add '__dict__' to the sequence of strings in the _ _ slots _ _ declaration.

- Without a _ _ weakref _ _ variable for each instance, classes defining _ _ slots _ _ do not support weak references to its instances. If weak reference support is needed, then add '__weakref__' to the sequence of strings in the _ _ slots _ _ declaration.

- _ _ slots _ _ are implemented at the class level by creating descriptors (3.3.2 *Implementing Descriptors*, page 36) for each variable name. As a result, class attributes cannot be used to set default values for instance variables defined by _ _ slots _ _ ; otherwise, the class attribute would overwrite the descriptor assignment.

- The action of a _ _ slots _ _ declaration is limited to the class where it is defined. As a result, subclasses will have a _ _ dict _ _ unless they also define _ _ slots _ _ (which must only contain names of any *additional* slots).

- If a class defines a slot also defined in a base class, the instance variable defined by the base class slot is inaccessible (except by retrieving its descriptor directly from the base class). This renders the meaning of the program undefined. In the future, a check may be added to prevent this.

- Nonempty _ _ *slots* _ _ does not work for classes derived from "variable-length" built-in types such as int, str and tuple.

- Any non-string iterable may be assigned to _ _ *slots* _ _ . Mappings may also be used; however, in the future, special meaning may be assigned to the values corresponding to each key.

- _ _ *class* _ _ assignment works only if both classes have the same _ _ *slots* _ _ .

3.3.3. Customizing class creation

By default, classes are constructed using type(). A class definition is read into a separate namespace and the value of class name is bound to the result of type(name, bases, dict).

When the class definition is read, if a callable metaclass keyword argument is passed after the bases in the class definition, the callable given will be called instead of type(). If other keyword arguments are passed, they will also be passed to the metaclass. This allows classes or functions to be written which monitor or alter the class creation process:

- Modifying the class dictionary prior to the class being created.

- Returning an instance of another class – essentially performing the role of a factory function.

These steps will have to be performed in the metaclass's __new__() method – type.__new__() can then be called from this method to create a class with different properties. This example adds a new element to the class dictionary before creating the class:

```
class metacls(type):
    def __new__(mcs, name, bases, dict):
        dict['foo'] = 'metacls was here'
        return type.__new__(mcs, name, bases, dict)
```

You can of course also override other class methods (or add new methods); for example defining a custom __call__() method in the metaclass allows custom behavior when the class is called, e.g. not always creating a new instance.

If the metaclass has a __prepare__() attribute (usually implemented as a class or static method), it is called before the class body is evaluated with the name of the class and a tuple of its bases for arguments. It should return an object that supports the mapping interface that will be used to store the namespace of the class. The default is a plain dictionary. This could be used, for example, to keep track of the order that class attributes are declared in by returning an ordered dictionary.

The appropriate metaclass is determined by the following precedence rules:

- If the metaclass keyword argument is passed with the bases, it is used.

- Otherwise, if there is at least one base class, its metaclass is used.

- Otherwise, the default metaclass (type) is used.

The potential uses for metaclasses are boundless. Some ideas that have been explored including logging, interface checking, automatic delegation, automatic property creation, proxies, frameworks, and automatic resource locking/synchronization.

Here is an example of a metaclass that uses an collections.OrderedDict to remember the order that class members were defined:

```
class OrderedClass(type):

    @classmethod
    def __prepare__(metacls, name, bases, **kwds):
        return collections.OrderedDict()

    def __new__(cls, name, bases, classdict):
        result = type.__new__(cls, name, bases, dict(classdict))
        result.members = tuple(classdict)
        return result

class A(metaclass=OrderedClass):
    def one(self): pass
    def two(self): pass
    def three(self): pass
    def four(self): pass

>>> A.members
('__module__', 'one', 'two', 'three', 'four')
```

When the class definition for *A* gets executed, the process begins with calling the metaclass's __prepare__() method which returns an empty collections.OrderedDict. That mapping records the methods and attributes of *A* as they are defined within the body of the class statement. Once those definitions are executed, the ordered dictionary is fully populated and the metaclass's __new__() method gets invoked. That method builds the new type and it saves the ordered dictionary keys in an attribute called members.

3.3.4. Customizing instance and subclass checks

The following methods are used to override the default behavior of the isinstance() and issubclass() built-in functions.

In particular, the metaclass abc.ABCMeta implements these methods in order to allow the addition of Abstract Base Classes (ABCs) as "virtual base classes" to any class or type (including built-in types), including other ABCs.

class.__instancecheck__(*self, instance*)
> Return true if *instance* should be considered a (direct or indirect) instance of *class*. If defined, called to implement isinstance(instance, class).

class.__subclasscheck__(*self, subclass*)
> Return true if *subclass* should be considered a (direct or indirect) subclass of *class*. If defined, called to implement issubclass(subclass, class).

Note that these methods are looked up on the type (metaclass) of a class. They cannot be defined as class methods in the actual class. This is consistent with the lookup of special methods that are called on instances, only in this case the instance is itself a class.

See Also:

PEP 3119[2] **- Introducing Abstract Base Classes** Includes the specification for customizing isinstance() and issubclass() behavior through __instancecheck__() and __subclasscheck__(), with motivation for this functionality in the context of adding Abstract Base Classes (see the abc module) to the language.

3.3.5. Emulating callable objects

object.__call__(*self*[, *args...*])
> Called when the instance is "called" as a function; if this method is defined, x(arg1, arg2, ...) is a shorthand for x.__call__(arg1, arg2, ...).

3.3.6. Emulating container types

The following methods can be defined to implement container objects. Containers usually are sequences (such as lists or tuples) or mappings (like dictionaries), but can represent other containers as well.

The first set of methods is used either to emulate a sequence or to emulate a mapping; the difference is that for a sequence, the allowable keys should be the integers k for which $0 <= k < N$ where N is the length of the sequence, or slice objects, which define a range of items. It is also recommended that mappings provide the methods keys(), values(), items(), get(), clear(), setdefault(), pop(), popitem(), copy(), and update() behaving similar to those for Python's standard dictionary objects. The collections module provides a MutableMapping abstract base class to help create those methods from a base set of __getitem__(), __setitem__(), __delitem__(), and keys().

Mutable sequences should provide methods append(), count(), index(), extend(), insert(), pop(), remove(), reverse() and sort(), like Python

---

[2]http://www.python.org/dev/peps/pep-3119

standard list objects. Finally, sequence types should implement addition (meaning concatenation) and multiplication (meaning repetition) by defining the methods __add__(), __radd__(), __iadd__(), __mul__(), __rmul__() and __imul__() described below; they should not define other numerical operators.

It is recommended that both mappings and sequences implement the __contains__() method to allow efficient use of the in operator; for mappings, in should search the mapping's keys; for sequences, it should search through the values. It is further recommended that both mappings and sequences implement the __iter__() method to allow efficient iteration through the container; for mappings, __iter__() should be the same as keys(); for sequences, it should iterate through the values.

object.__len__(*self*)

Called to implement the built-in function len(). Should return the length of the object, an integer >= 0. Also, an object that doesn't define a __bool__() method and whose __len__() method returns zero is considered to be false in a Boolean context.

Note: Slicing is done exclusively with the following three methods. A call like

a[1:2] = b

is translated to

a[slice(1, 2, None)] = b

and so forth. Missing slice items are always filled in with None.

object.__getitem__(*self, key*)

Called to implement evaluation of self[key]. For sequence types, the accepted keys should be integers and slice objects. Note that the special interpretation of negative indexes (if the class wishes to emulate a sequence type) is up to the __getitem__() method. If *key* is of an inappropriate type, TypeError may be raised; if of a value outside the set of indexes for the sequence (after any special interpretation of negative values), IndexError should be raised. For mapping types, if *key* is missing (not in the container), KeyError should be raised.

Note: for loops expect that an IndexError will be raised for illegal indexes to allow proper detection of the end of the sequence.

object.__setitem__(*self, key, value*)

Called to implement assignment to self[key]. Same note as for __getitem__(). This should only be implemented for mappings if the objects support changes to the values for keys, or if new keys can be added, or for sequences if elements can be replaced. The same exceptions should be raised for improper *key* values as for the __getitem__() method.

object.__delitem__(*self, key*)

Called to implement deletion of self[key]. Same note as for __getitem__(). This should only be implemented for mappings if the objects support removal of keys, or for sequences if elements can be removed from the sequence. The same exceptions should be raised for improper *key* values as for the `__getitem__()` method.

`object.__iter__(`*self*`)`

This method is called when an iterator is required for a container. This method should return a new iterator object that can iterate over all the objects in the container. For mappings, it should iterate over the keys of the container, and should also be made available as the method `keys()`.

Iterator objects also need to implement this method; they are required to return themselves. For more information on iterator objects, see *Iterator Types* in "The Python Library Reference Manual".

`object.__reversed__(`*self*`)`

Called (if present) by the `reversed()` built-in to implement reverse iteration. It should return a new iterator object that iterates over all the objects in the container in reverse order.

If the `__reversed__()` method is not provided, the `reversed()` built-in will fall back to using the sequence protocol (`__len__()` and `__getitem__()`). Objects that support the sequence protocol should only provide `__reversed__()` if they can provide an implementation that is more efficient than the one provided by `reversed()`.

The membership test operators (in and not in) are normally implemented as an iteration through a sequence. However, container objects can supply the following special method with a more efficient implementation, which also does not require the object be a sequence.

`object.__contains__(`*self, item*`)`

Called to implement membership test operators. Should return true if *item* is in *self*, false otherwise. For mapping objects, this should consider the keys of the mapping rather than the values or the key-item pairs.

For objects that don't define `__contains__()`, the membership test first tries iteration via `__iter__()`, then the old sequence iteration protocol via `__getitem__()`, see 5.9 *Comparisons* (page 68).

3.3.7. Emulating numeric types

The following methods can be defined to emulate numeric objects. Methods corresponding to operations that are not supported by the particular kind of number implemented (e.g., bitwise operations for non-integral numbers) should be left undefined.

`object.__add__(`*self, other*`)`
`object.__sub__(`*self, other*`)`
`object.__mul__(`*self, other*`)`
`object.__truediv__(`*self, other*`)`
`object.__floordiv__(`*self, other*`)`

```
object.__mod__(self, other)
object.__divmod__(self, other)
object.__pow__(self, other[, modulo])
object.__lshift__(self, other)
object.__rshift__(self, other)
object.__and__(self, other)
object.__xor__(self, other)
object.__or__(self, other)
```

These methods are called to implement the binary arithmetic operations (+, -, *, /, //, %, divmod(), pow(), **, <<, >>, &, ^, |). For instance, to evaluate the expression x + y, where x is an instance of a class that has an __add__() method, x.__add__(y) is called. The __divmod__() method should be the equivalent to using __floordiv__() and __mod__(); it should not be related to __truediv__(). Note that __pow__() should be defined to accept an optional third argument if the ternary version of the built-in pow() function is to be supported.

If one of those methods does not support the operation with the supplied arguments, it should return NotImplemented.

```
object.__radd__(self, other)
object.__rsub__(self, other)
object.__rmul__(self, other)
object.__rtruediv__(self, other)
object.__rfloordiv__(self, other)
object.__rmod__(self, other)
object.__rdivmod__(self, other)
object.__rpow__(self, other)
object.__rlshift__(self, other)
object.__rrshift__(self, other)
object.__rand__(self, other)
object.__rxor__(self, other)
object.__ror__(self, other)
```

These methods are called to implement the binary arithmetic operations (+, -, *, /, //, %, divmod(), pow(), **, <<, >>, &, ^, |) with reflected (swapped) operands. These functions are only called if the left operand does not support the corresponding operation and the operands are of different types.[3] For instance, to evaluate the expression x - y, where y is an instance of a class that has an __rsub__() method, y.__rsub__(x) is called if x.__sub__(y) returns *NotImplemented*.

Note that ternary pow() will not try calling __rpow__() (the coercion rules would become too complicated).

Note: If the right operand's type is a subclass of the left operand's type and that subclass provides the reflected method for the operation, this method

---

[3]For operands of the same type, it is assumed that if the non-reflected method (such as __add__()) fails the operation is not supported, which is why the reflected method is not called.

will be called before the left operand's non-reflected method. This behavior allows subclasses to override their ancestors' operations.

object.__iadd__(*self*, *other*)
object.__isub__(*self*, *other*)
object.__imul__(*self*, *other*)
object.__itruediv__(*self*, *other*)
object.__ifloordiv__(*self*, *other*)
object.__imod__(*self*, *other*)
object.__ipow__(*self*, *other*[, *modulo*])
object.__ilshift__(*self*, *other*)
object.__irshift__(*self*, *other*)
object.__iand__(*self*, *other*)
object.__ixor__(*self*, *other*)
object.__ior__(*self*, *other*)

These methods are called to implement the augmented arithmetic assignments (+=, -=, *=, /=, //=, %=, **=, <<=, >>=, &=, ^=, |=). These methods should attempt to do the operation in-place (modifying *self*) and return the result (which could be, but does not have to be, *self*). If a specific method is not defined, the augmented assignment falls back to the normal methods. For instance, to execute the statement x += y, where *x* is an instance of a class that has an __iadd__() method, x.__iadd__(y) is called. If *x* is an instance of a class that does not define a __iadd__() method, x.__add__(y) and y.__radd__(x) are considered, as with the evaluation of x + y.

object.__neg__(*self*)
object.__pos__(*self*)
object.__abs__(*self*)
object.__invert__(*self*)

Called to implement the unary arithmetic operations (-, +, abs() and ~).

object.__complex__(*self*)
object.__int__(*self*)
object.__float__(*self*)
object.__round__(*self*[, *n*])

Called to implement the built-in functions complex(), int(), float() and round(). Should return a value of the appropriate type.

object.__index__(*self*)

Called to implement operator.index(). Also called whenever Python needs an integer object (such as in slicing, or in the built-in bin(), hex() and oct() functions). Must return an integer.

3.3.8. With Statement Context Managers

A *context manager* is an object that defines the runtime context to be established when executing a with statement. The context manager handles the entry into, and the exit from, the desired runtime context for the execution of the block of code. Context managers are normally invoked using the with statement (described in section 7.5 *The with statement*, page 93), but can also be used by directly invoking their methods.

Typical uses of context managers include saving and restoring various kinds of global state, locking and unlocking resources, closing opened files, etc.

For more information on context managers, see *Context Manager Types* in "The Python Library Reference Manual".

object.__enter__(*self*)
> Enter the runtime context related to this object. The with statement will bind this method's return value to the target(s) specified in the as clause of the statement, if any.

object.__exit__(*self, exc_type, exc_value, traceback*)
> Exit the runtime context related to this object. The parameters describe the exception that caused the context to be exited. If the context was exited without an exception, all three arguments will be None.
>
> If an exception is supplied, and the method wishes to suppress the exception (i.e., prevent it from being propagated), it should return a true value. Otherwise, the exception will be processed normally upon exit from this method.
>
> Note that __exit__() methods should not reraise the passed-in exception; this is the caller's responsibility.

See Also:

PEP 0343[4] **- The "with" statement** The specification, background, and examples for the Python with statement.

3.3.9. Special method lookup

For custom classes, implicit invocations of special methods are only guaranteed to work correctly if defined on an object's type, not in the object's instance dictionary. That behaviour is the reason why the following code raises an exception:

```
>>> class C:
...     pass
...
>>> c = C()
>>> c.__len__ = lambda: 5
>>> len(c)
Traceback (most recent call last):
  File "<stdin>", line 1, in <module>
TypeError: object of type 'C' has no len()
```

The rationale behind this behaviour lies with a number of special methods such as __hash__() and __repr__() that are implemented by all objects, including

---

[4]http://www.python.org/dev/peps/pep-0343

type objects. If the implicit lookup of these methods used the conventional lookup process, they would fail when invoked on the type object itself:

```
>>> 1 .__hash__() == hash(1)
True
>>> int.__hash__() == hash(int)
Traceback (most recent call last):
  File "<stdin>", line 1, in <module>
TypeError: descriptor '__hash__' of 'int' object needs an argument
```

Incorrectly attempting to invoke an unbound method of a class in this way is sometimes referred to as 'metaclass confusion', and is avoided by bypassing the instance when looking up special methods:

```
>>> type(1).__hash__(1) == hash(1)
True
>>> type(int).__hash__(int) == hash(int)
True
```

In addition to bypassing any instance attributes in the interest of correctness, implicit special method lookup generally also bypasses the __getattribute__() method even of the object's metaclass:

```
>>> class Meta(type):
...     def __getattribute__(*args):
...         print("Metaclass getattribute invoked")
...         return type.__getattribute__(*args)
...
>>> class C(object, metaclass=Meta):
...     def __len__(self):
...         return 10
...     def __getattribute__(*args):
...         print("Class getattribute invoked")
...         return object.__getattribute__(*args)
...
>>> c = C()
>>> c.__len__()                 # Explicit lookup via instance
Class getattribute invoked
10
>>> type(c).__len__(c)          # Explicit lookup via type
Metaclass getattribute invoked
10
>>> len(c)                      # Implicit lookup
10
```

Bypassing the __getattribute__() machinery in this fashion provides significant scope for speed optimisations within the interpreter, at the cost of some flexibility in the handling of special methods (the special method *must* be set on the class object itself in order to be consistently invoked by the interpreter).

4. Execution model

4.1. Naming and binding

Names refer to objects. Names are introduced by name binding operations. Each occurrence of a name in the program text refers to the *binding* of that name established in the innermost function block containing the use.

A *block* is a piece of Python program text that is executed as a unit. The following are blocks: a module, a function body, and a class definition. Each command typed interactively is a block. A script file (a file given as standard input to the interpreter or specified on the interpreter command line the first argument) is a code block. A script command (a command specified on the interpreter command line with the '-c' option) is a code block. The string argument passed to the built-in functions eval() and exec() is a code block.

A code block is executed in an *execution frame*. A frame contains some administrative information (used for debugging) and determines where and how execution continues after the code block's execution has completed.

A *scope* defines the visibility of a name within a block. If a local variable is defined in a block, its scope includes that block. If the definition occurs in a function block, the scope extends to any blocks contained within the defining one, unless a contained block introduces a different binding for the name. The scope of names defined in a class block is limited to the class block; it does not extend to the code blocks of methods – this includes comprehensions and generator expressions since they are implemented using a function scope. This means that the following will fail:

```
class A:
    a = 42
    b = list(a + i for i in range(10))
```

When a name is used in a code block, it is resolved using the nearest enclosing scope. The set of all such scopes visible to a code block is called the block's *environment*.

If a name is bound in a block, it is a local variable of that block, unless declared as nonlocal. If a name is bound at the module level, it is a global variable. (The variables of the module code block are local and global.) If a variable is used in a code block but not defined there, it is a *free variable*.

When a name is not found at all, a NameError exception is raised. If the name refers to a local variable that has not been bound, a UnboundLocalError exception is raised. UnboundLocalError is a subclass of NameError.

The following constructs bind names: formal parameters to functions, import statements, class and function definitions (these bind the class or function name in the defining block), and targets that are identifiers if occurring in an assignment, for loop header, or after as in a with statement or except clause. The import statement of the form from ... import * binds all names defined in the imported module, except those beginning with an underscore. This form may only be used at the module level.

A target occurring in a del statement is also considered bound for this purpose (though the actual semantics are to unbind the name). It is illegal to unbind a name that is referenced by an enclosing scope; the compiler will report a SyntaxError.

Each assignment or import statement occurs within a block defined by a class or function definition or at the module level (the top-level code block).

If a name binding operation occurs anywhere within a code block, all uses of the name within the block are treated as references to the current block. This can lead to errors when a name is used within a block before it is bound. This rule is subtle. Python lacks declarations and allows name binding operations to occur anywhere within a code block. The local variables of a code block can be determined by scanning the entire text of the block for name binding operations.

If the global statement occurs within a block, all uses of the name specified in the statement refer to the binding of that name in the top-level namespace. Names are resolved in the top-level namespace by searching the global namespace, i.e. the namespace of the module containing the code block, and the builtins namespace, the namespace of the module builtins. The global namespace is searched first. If the name is not found there, the builtins namespace is searched. The global statement must precede all uses of the name.

The builtins namespace associated with the execution of a code block is actually found by looking up the name __builtins__ in its global namespace; this should be a dictionary or a module (in the latter case the module's dictionary is used). By default, when in the __main__ module, __builtins__ is the built-in module builtins; when in any other module, __builtins__ is an alias for the dictionary of the builtins module itself. __builtins__ can be set to a user-created dictionary to create a weak form of restricted execution.

CPython implementation detail: Users should not touch __builtins__; it is strictly an implementation detail. Users wanting to override values in the builtins namespace should import the builtins module and modify its attributes appropriately.

The namespace for a module is automatically created the first time a module is imported. The main module for a script is always called __main__.

The global statement has the same scope as a name binding operation in the same block. If the nearest enclosing scope for a free variable contains a global statement, the free variable is treated as a global.

A class definition is an executable statement that may use and define names. These references follow the normal rules for name resolution. The namespace of the class definition becomes the attribute dictionary of the class. Names defined at the class scope are not visible in methods.

4.1.1. Interaction with dynamic features

There are several cases where Python statements are illegal when used in conjunction with nested scopes that contain free variables.

If a variable is referenced in an enclosing scope, it is illegal to delete the name. An error will be reported at compile time.

If the wild card form of import — import * — is used in a function and the function contains or is a nested block with free variables, the compiler will raise a SyntaxError.

The eval() and exec() functions do not have access to the full environment for resolving names. Names may be resolved in the local and global namespaces of the caller. Free variables are not resolved in the nearest enclosing namespace, but in the global namespace.[1] The exec() and eval() functions have optional arguments to override the global and local namespace. If only one namespace is specified, it is used for both.

4.2. Exceptions

Exceptions are a means of breaking out of the normal flow of control of a code block in order to handle errors or other exceptional conditions. An exception is *raised* at the point where the error is detected; it may be *handled* by the surrounding code block or by any code block that directly or indirectly invoked the code block where the error occurred.

The Python interpreter raises an exception when it detects a run-time error (such as division by zero). A Python program can also explicitly raise an exception with the raise statement. Exception handlers are specified with the try ... except statement. The finally clause of such a statement can be used to specify cleanup code which does not handle the exception, but is executed whether an exception occurred or not in the preceding code.

Python uses the "termination" model of error handling: an exception handler can find out what happened and continue execution at an outer level, but it cannot repair the cause of the error and retry the failing operation (except by re-entering the offending piece of code from the top).

When an exception is not handled at all, the interpreter terminates execution of the program, or returns to its interactive main loop. In either case, it prints a stack backtrace, except when the exception is SystemExit.

---

[1]This limitation occurs because the code that is executed by these operations is not available at the time the module is compiled.

Exceptions are identified by class instances. The except clause is selected depending on the class of the instance: it must reference the class of the instance or a base class thereof. The instance can be received by the handler and can carry additional information about the exceptional condition.

Note: Exception messages are not part of the Python API. Their contents may change from one version of Python to the next without warning and should not be relied on by code which will run under multiple versions of the interpreter.

See also the description of the try statement in section 7.4 *The try statement* (page 91) and raise statement in section 6.8 *The raise statement* (page 79).

5. Expressions

This chapter explains the meaning of the elements of expressions in Python.

Syntax Notes: In this and the following chapters, extended BNF notation will be used to describe syntax, not lexical analysis. When (one alternative of) a syntax rule has the form

    name   ::= othername

and no semantics are given, the semantics of this form of name are the same as for othername.

5.1. Arithmetic conversions

When a description of an arithmetic operator below uses the phrase "the numeric arguments are converted to a common type," this means that the operator implementation for built-in types works that way:

- If either argument is a complex number, the other is converted to complex;
- otherwise, if either argument is a floating point number, the other is converted to floating point;
- otherwise, both must be integers and no conversion is necessary.

Some additional rules apply for certain operators (e.g., a string left argument to the '%' operator). Extensions must define their own conversion behavior.

5.2. Atoms

Atoms are the most basic elements of expressions. The simplest atoms are identifiers or literals. Forms enclosed in parentheses, brackets or braces are also categorized syntactically as atoms. The syntax for atoms is:

    atom   ::= identifier | literal | enclosure
    enclosure ::= parenth_form | list_display | dict_display |
                    set_display
                    | generator_expression | yield_atom

5.2.1. Identifiers (Names)

An identifier occurring as an atom is a name. See section 2.3 *Identifiers and keywords* (page 11) for lexical definition and section 4.1 *Naming and binding* (page 49) for documentation of naming and binding.

When the name is bound to an object, evaluation of the atom yields that object. When a name is not bound, an attempt to evaluate it raises a NameError exception.

Private name mangling: When an identifier that textually occurs in a class definition begins with two or more underscore characters and does not end in two or more underscores, it is considered a *private name* of that class. Private names are transformed to a longer form before code is generated for them. The transformation inserts the class name in front of the name, with leading underscores removed, and a single underscore inserted in front of the class name. For example, the identifier __spam occurring in a class named Ham will be transformed to _Ham__spam. This transformation is independent of the syntactical context in which the identifier is used. If the transformed name is extremely long (longer than 255 characters), implementation defined truncation may happen. If the class name consists only of underscores, no transformation is done.

5.2.2. Literals

Python supports string and bytes literals and various numeric literals:

```
literal   ::=   stringliteral | bytesliteral
              | integer | floatnumber | imagnumber
```

Evaluation of a literal yields an object of the given type (string, bytes, integer, floating point number, complex number) with the given value. The value may be approximated in the case of floating point and imaginary (complex) literals. See section 2.4 *Literals* (page 13) for details.

With the exception of bytes literals, these all correspond to immutable data types, and hence the object's identity is less important than its value. Multiple evaluations of literals with the same value (either the same occurrence in the program text or a different occurrence) may obtain the same object or a different object with the same value.

5.2.3. Parenthesized forms

A parenthesized form is an optional expression list enclosed in parentheses:

```
parenth_form   ::=   "(" [expression_list] ")"
```

A parenthesized expression list yields whatever that expression list yields: if the list contains at least one comma, it yields a tuple; otherwise, it yields the single expression that makes up the expression list.

An empty pair of parentheses yields an empty tuple object. Since tuples are immutable, the rules for literals apply (i.e., two occurrences of the empty tuple may or may not yield the same object).

Note that tuples are not formed by the parentheses, but rather by use of the comma operator. The exception is the empty tuple, for which parentheses *are* required — allowing unparenthesized "nothing" in expressions would cause ambiguities and allow common typos to pass uncaught.

5.2.4. Displays for lists, sets and dictionaries

For constructing a list, a set or a dictionary Python provides special syntax called "displays", each of them in two flavors:

- either the container contents are listed explicitly, or
- they are computed via a set of looping and filtering instructions, called a *comprehension.*

Common syntax elements for comprehensions are:

```
comprehension   ::=   expression comp_for
comp_for        ::=   "for" target_list "in" or_test
                      [comp_iter]
comp_iter       ::=   comp_for | comp_if
comp_if         ::=   "if" expression_nocond [comp_iter]
```

The comprehension consists of a single expression followed by at least one for clause and zero or more for or if clauses. In this case, the elements of the new container are those that would be produced by considering each of the for or if clauses a block, nesting from left to right, and evaluating the expression to produce an element each time the innermost block is reached.

Note that the comprehension is executed in a separate scope, so names assigned to in the target list don't "leak" in the enclosing scope.

5.2.5. List displays

A list display is a possibly empty series of expressions enclosed in square brackets:

```
list_display   ::=   "[" [expression_list | comprehension] "]"
```

A list display yields a new list object, the contents being specified by either a list of expressions or a comprehension. When a comma-separated list of expressions is supplied, its elements are evaluated from left to right and placed into the list object in that order. When a comprehension is supplied, the list is constructed from the elements resulting from the comprehension.

5.2.6. Set displays

A set display is denoted by curly braces and distinguishable from dictionary displays by the lack of colons separating keys and values:

```
set_display   ::=   "{" (expression_list | comprehension) "}"
```

A set display yields a new mutable set object, the contents being specified by either a sequence of expressions or a comprehension. When a comma-separated list of expressions is supplied, its elements are evaluated from left to right and added to the set object. When a comprehension is supplied, the set is constructed from the elements resulting from the comprehension.

An empty set cannot be constructed with {}; this literal constructs an empty dictionary.

5.2.7. Dictionary displays

A dictionary display is a possibly empty series of key/datum pairs enclosed in curly braces:

```
dict_display          ::=  "{" [key_datum_list |
                           dict_comprehension] "}"
key_datum_list        ::=  key_datum ("," key_datum)* [","]
key_datum             ::=  expression ":" expression
dict_comprehension    ::=  expression ":" expression comp_for
```

A dictionary display yields a new dictionary object.

If a comma-separated sequence of key/datum pairs is given, they are evaluated from left to right to define the entries of the dictionary: each key object is used as a key into the dictionary to store the corresponding datum. This means that you can specify the same key multiple times in the key/datum list, and the final dictionary's value for that key will be the last one given.

A dict comprehension, in contrast to list and set comprehensions, needs two expressions separated with a colon followed by the usual "for" and "if" clauses. When the comprehension is run, the resulting key and value elements are inserted in the new dictionary in the order they are produced.

Restrictions on the types of the key values are listed earlier in section 3.2 *The standard type hierarchy* (page 20). (To summarize, the key type should be *hashable*, which excludes all mutable objects.) Clashes between duplicate keys are not detected; the last datum (textually rightmost in the display) stored for a given key value prevails.

5.2.8. Generator expressions

A generator expression is a compact generator notation in parentheses:

```
generator_expression   ::=   "(" expression comp_for ")"
```

A generator expression yields a new generator object. Its syntax is the same as for comprehensions, except that it is enclosed in parentheses instead of brackets or curly braces.

Variables used in the generator expression are evaluated lazily when the __next__() method is called for generator object (in the same fashion as normal generators). However, the leftmost for clause is immediately evaluated, so that an error produced by it can be seen before any other possible error in the code that handles the generator expression. Subsequent for clauses cannot be evaluated immediately since they may depend on the previous for loop. For example: (x*y for x in range(10) for y in bar(x)).

The parentheses can be omitted on calls with only one argument. See section 5.3.4 *Calls* (page 61) for the detail.

5.2.9. Yield expressions

```
yield_atom        ::=  "(" yield_expression ")"
yield_expression  ::=  "yield" [expression_list]
```

The yield expression is only used when defining a generator function, and can only be used in the body of a function definition. Using a yield expression in a function definition is sufficient to cause that definition to create a generator function instead of a normal function.

When a generator function is called, it returns an iterator known as a generator. That generator then controls the execution of a generator function. The execution starts when one of the generator's methods is called. At that time, the execution proceeds to the first yield expression, where it is suspended again, returning the value of expression_list to generator's caller. By suspended we mean that all local state is retained, including the current bindings of local variables, the instruction pointer, and the internal evaluation stack. When the execution is resumed by calling one of the generator's methods, the function can proceed exactly as if the yield expression was just another external call. The value of the yield expression after resuming depends on the method which resumed the execution.

All of this makes generator functions quite similar to coroutines; they yield multiple times, they have more than one entry point and their execution can be suspended. The only difference is that a generator function cannot control where should the execution continue after it yields; the control is always transferred to the generator's caller.

The yield statement is allowed in the try clause of a try ... finally construct. If the generator is not resumed before it is finalized (by reaching a zero reference count or by being garbage collected), the generator-iterator's close() method will be called, allowing any pending finally clauses to execute.

The following generator's methods can be used to control the execution of a generator function:

generator.__next__()
   Starts the execution of a generator function or resumes it at the last executed yield expression. When a generator function is resumed with a __next__() method, the current yield expression always evaluates to None. The execution then continues to the next yield expression, where the generator is suspended again, and the value of the expression_list is returned to next()'s caller. If the generator exits without yielding another value, a StopIteration exception is raised.

   This method is normally called implicitly, e.g. by a for loop, or by the built-in next() function.

`generator.send(`*value*`)`

Resumes the execution and "sends" a value into the generator function. The value argument becomes the result of the current `yield` expression. The `send()` method returns the next value yielded by the generator, or raises `StopIteration` if the generator exits without yielding another value. When `send()` is called to start the generator, it must be called with `None` as the argument, because there is no `yield` expression that could receive the value.

`generator.throw(`*type*`[, `*value*`[, `*traceback*`]])`

Raises an exception of type type at the point where generator was paused, and returns the next value yielded by the generator function. If the generator exits without yielding another value, a `StopIteration` exception is raised. If the generator function does not catch the passed-in exception, or raises a different exception, then that exception propagates to the caller.

`generator.close()`

Raises a `GeneratorExit` at the point where the generator function was paused. If the generator function then raises `StopIteration` (by exiting normally, or due to already being closed) or `GeneratorExit` (by not catching the exception), close returns to its caller. If the generator yields a value, a `RuntimeError` is raised. If the generator raises any other exception, it is propagated to the caller. `close()` does nothing if the generator has already exited due to an exception or normal exit.

Here is a simple example that demonstrates the behavior of generators and generator functions:

```
>>> def echo(value=None):
...     print("Execution starts when 'next()' is called for the
first time.")
...     try:
...         while True:
...             try:
...                 value = (yield value)
...             except Exception as e:
...                 value = e
...     finally:
...         print("Don't forget to clean up when 'close()' is
called.")
...
>>> generator = echo(1)
>>> print(next(generator))
Execution starts when 'next()' is called for the first time.
1
>>> print(next(generator))
None
>>> print(generator.send(2))
2
```

```
>>> generator.throw(TypeError, "spam")
TypeError('spam',)
>>> generator.close()
Don't forget to clean up when 'close()' is called.
```

See Also:

PEP 0255[1] **- Simple Generators** The proposal for adding generators and
the yield statement to Python.

PEP 0342[2] **- Coroutines via Enhanced Generators** The proposal to
enhance the API and syntax of generators, making them usable as simple
coroutines.

5.3. Primaries

Primaries represent the most tightly bound operations of the language. Their
syntax is:

```
primary  ::=  atom | attributeref | subscription | slicing |
              call
```

5.3.1. Attribute references

An attribute reference is a primary followed by a period and a name:

```
attributeref  ::=  primary "." identifier
```

The primary must evaluate to an object of a type that supports attribute references, which most objects do. This object is then asked to produce the attribute whose name is the identifier (which can be customized by overriding
the __getattr__() method). If this attribute is not available, the exception
AttributeError is raised. Otherwise, the type and value of the object produced is determined by the object. Multiple evaluations of the same attribute
reference may yield different objects.

5.3.2. Subscriptions

A subscription selects an item of a sequence (string, tuple or list) or mapping
(dictionary) object:

```
subscription  ::=  primary "[" expression_list "]"
```

The primary must evaluate to an object that supports subscription, e.g. a
list or dictionary. User-defined objects can support subscription by defining
a __getitem__() method.

For built-in objects, there are two types of objects that support subscription:

---

[1]http://www.python.org/dev/peps/pep-0255
[2]http://www.python.org/dev/peps/pep-0342

If the primary is a mapping, the expression list must evaluate to an object whose value is one of the keys of the mapping, and the subscription selects the value in the mapping that corresponds to that key. (The expression list is a tuple except if it has exactly one item.)

If the primary is a sequence, the expression (list) must evaluate to an integer or a slice (as discussed in the following section).

The formal syntax makes no special provision for negative indices in sequences; however, built-in sequences all provide a __getitem__() method that interprets negative indices by adding the length of the sequence to the index (so that x[-1] selects the last item of x). The resulting value must be a nonnegative integer less than the number of items in the sequence, and the subscription selects the item whose index is that value (counting from zero). Since the support for negative indices and slicing occurs in the object's __getitem__() method, subclasses overriding this method will need to explicitly add that support.

A string's items are characters. A character is not a separate data type but a string of exactly one character.

5.3.3. Slicings

A slicing selects a range of items in a sequence object (e.g., a string, tuple or list). Slicings may be used as expressions or as targets in assignment or del statements. The syntax for a slicing:

```
slicing        ::=  primary "[" slice_list "]"
slice_list     ::=  slice_item ("," slice_item)* [","]
slice_item     ::=  expression | proper_slice
proper_slice   ::=  [lower_bound] ":" [upper_bound] [ ":"
                    [stride] ]
lower_bound    ::=  expression
upper_bound    ::=  expression
stride         ::=  expression
```

There is ambiguity in the formal syntax here: anything that looks like an expression list also looks like a slice list, so any subscription can be interpreted as a slicing. Rather than further complicating the syntax, this is disambiguated by defining that in this case the interpretation as a subscription takes priority over the interpretation as a slicing (this is the case if the slice list contains no proper slice).

The semantics for a slicing are as follows. The primary must evaluate to a mapping object, and it is indexed (using the same __getitem__() method as normal subscription) with a key that is constructed from the slice list, as follows. If the slice list contains at least one comma, the key is a tuple containing the conversion of the slice items; otherwise, the conversion of the lone slice item is the key. The conversion of a slice item that is an expression is that expression. The conversion of a proper slice is a slice object (see section 3.2 *The standard type hierarchy*, page 20) whose start, stop and step attributes are the values of the expressions given as lower bound, upper bound and stride, respectively, substituting None for missing expressions.

5.3.4. Calls

A call calls a callable object (e.g., a function) with a possibly empty series of arguments:

```
call                    ::=  primary "(" [argument_list [","] |
                             comprehension] ")"
argument_list           ::=  positional_arguments [","
                             keyword_arguments]
                             [","  "*" expression] [","
                             keyword_arguments]
                             [","  "**" expression]
                             | keyword_arguments [","  "*"
                             expression]
                             [","  keyword_arguments] [","  "**"
                             expression]
                             | "*" expression [","
                             keyword_arguments] [","  "**"
                             expression]
                             | "**" expression
positional_arguments    ::=  expression ("," expression)*
keyword_arguments       ::=  keyword_item ("," keyword_item)*
keyword_item            ::=  identifier "=" expression
```

A trailing comma may be present after the positional and keyword arguments but does not affect the semantics.

The primary must evaluate to a callable object (user-defined functions, built-in functions, methods of built-in objects, class objects, methods of class instances, and all objects having a __call__() method are callable). All argument expressions are evaluated before the call is attempted. Please refer to section 7.6 *Function definitions* (page 94) for the syntax of formal parameter lists.

If keyword arguments are present, they are first converted to positional arguments, as follows. First, a list of unfilled slots is created for the formal parameters. If there are N positional arguments, they are placed in the first N slots. Next, for each keyword argument, the identifier is used to determine the corresponding slot (if the identifier is the same as the first formal parameter name, the first slot is used, and so on). If the slot is already filled, a TypeError exception is raised. Otherwise, the value of the argument is placed in the slot, filling it (even if the expression is None, it fills the slot). When all arguments have been processed, the slots that are still unfilled are filled with the corresponding default value from the function definition. (Default values are calculated, once, when the function is defined; thus, a mutable object such as a list or dictionary used as default value will be shared by all calls that don't specify an argument value for the corresponding slot; this should usually be avoided.) If there are any unfilled slots for which no default value is specified, a `TypeError` exception is raised. Otherwise, the list of filled slots is used as the argument list for the call.

CPython implementation detail: An implementation may provide built-in functions whose positional parameters do not have names, even if they are 'named' for the purpose of documentation, and which therefore cannot be supplied by keyword. In CPython, this is the case for functions implemented in C that use `PyArg_ParseTuple()` to parse their arguments.

If there are more positional arguments than there are formal parameter slots, a `TypeError` exception is raised, unless a formal parameter using the syntax `*identifier` is present; in this case, that formal parameter receives a tuple containing the excess positional arguments (or an empty tuple if there were no excess positional arguments).

If any keyword argument does not correspond to a formal parameter name, a `TypeError` exception is raised, unless a formal parameter using the syntax `**identifier` is present; in this case, that formal parameter receives a dictionary containing the excess keyword arguments (using the keywords as keys and the argument values as corresponding values), or a (new) empty dictionary if there were no excess keyword arguments.

If the syntax `*expression` appears in the function call, `expression` must evaluate to a sequence. Elements from this sequence are treated as if they were additional positional arguments; if there are positional arguments $x1, \ldots, xN$, and `expression` evaluates to a sequence $y1, \ldots, yM$, this is equivalent to a call with M+N positional arguments $x1, \ldots, xN, y1, \ldots, yM$.

A consequence of this is that although the `*expression` syntax may appear *after* some keyword arguments, it is processed *before* the keyword arguments (and the `**expression` argument, if any – see below). So:

```
>>> def f(a, b):
...   print(a, b)
...
>>> f(b=1, *(2,))
2 1
>>> f(a=1, *(2,))
Traceback (most recent call last):
  File "<stdin>", line 1, in ?
TypeError: f() got multiple values for keyword argument 'a'
>>> f(1, *(2,))
1 2
```

It is unusual for both keyword arguments and the `*expression` syntax to be used in the same call, so in practice this confusion does not arise.

If the syntax `**expression` appears in the function call, `expression` must evaluate to a mapping, the contents of which are treated as additional keyword arguments. In the case of a keyword appearing in both expression and as an explicit keyword argument, a TypeError exception is raised.

Formal parameters using the syntax *identifier or **identifier cannot be used as positional argument slots or as keyword argument names.

A call always returns some value, possibly None, unless it raises an exception. How this value is computed depends on the type of the callable object.

If it is—

a user-defined function: The code block for the function is executed, passing it the argument list. The first thing the code block will do is bind the formal parameters to the arguments; this is described in section 7.6 *Function definitions* (page 94). When the code block executes a return statement, this specifies the return value of the function call.

a built-in function or method: The result is up to the interpreter; see *Built-in Functions* in "The Python Library Reference Manual" for the descriptions of built-in functions and methods.

a class object: A new instance of that class is returned.

a class instance method: The corresponding user-defined function is called, with an argument list that is one longer than the argument list of the call: the instance becomes the first argument.

a class instance: The class must define a __call__() method; the effect is then the same as if that method was called.

5.4. The power operator

The power operator binds more tightly than unary operators on its left; it binds less tightly than unary operators on its right. The syntax is:

```
power   ::=   primary ["**" u_expr]
```

Thus, in an unparenthesized sequence of power and unary operators, the operators are evaluated from right to left (this does not constrain the evaluation order for the operands): -1**2 results in -1.

The power operator has the same semantics as the built-in pow() function, when called with two arguments: it yields its left argument raised to the power of its right argument. The numeric arguments are first converted to a common type, and the result is of that type.

For int operands, the result has the same type as the operands unless the second argument is negative; in that case, all arguments are converted to float and a float result is delivered. For example, 10**2 returns 100, but 10**-2 returns 0.01.

Raising 0.0 to a negative power results in a ZeroDivisionError. Raising a negative number to a fractional power results in a complex number. (In earlier versions it raised a ValueError.)

5.5. Unary arithmetic and bitwise operations

All unary arithmetic and bitwise operations have the same priority:

```
u_expr  ::=  power | "-" u_expr | "+" u_expr | "~" u_expr
```

The unary - (minus) operator yields the negation of its numeric argument.

The unary + (plus) operator yields its numeric argument unchanged.

The unary ~ (invert) operator yields the bitwise inversion of its integer argument. The bitwise inversion of x is defined as -(x+1). It only applies to integral numbers.

In all three cases, if the argument does not have the proper type, a TypeError exception is raised.

5.6. Binary arithmetic operations

The binary arithmetic operations have the conventional priority levels. Note that some of these operations also apply to certain non-numeric types. Apart from the power operator, there are only two levels, one for multiplicative operators and one for additive operators:

```
m_expr  ::=  u_expr | m_expr "*" u_expr | m_expr "//" u_expr
          | m_expr "/" u_expr
          | m_expr "%" u_expr
a_expr  ::=  m_expr | a_expr "+" m_expr | a_expr "-" m_expr
```

The * (multiplication) operator yields the product of its arguments. The arguments must either both be numbers, or one argument must be an integer and the other must be a sequence. In the former case, the numbers are converted to a common type and then multiplied together. In the latter case, sequence repetition is performed; a negative repetition factor yields an empty sequence.

The / (division) and // (floor division) operators yield the quotient of their arguments. The numeric arguments are first converted to a common type. Integer division yields a float, while floor division of integers results in an integer; the result is that of mathematical division with the 'floor' function applied to the result. Division by zero raises the ZeroDivisionError exception.

The % (modulo) operator yields the remainder from the division of the first argument by the second. The numeric arguments are first converted to a common type. A zero right argument raises the ZeroDivisionError exception. The arguments may be floating point numbers, e.g., 3.14%0.7 equals 0.34 (since 3.14 equals 4*0.7 + 0.34). The modulo operator always yields a result with the same sign as its second operand (or zero); the absolute value of the result is strictly smaller than the absolute value of the second operand[3].

The floor division and modulo operators are connected by the following identity: `x == (x//y)*y + (x%y)`. Floor division and modulo are also connected with the built-in function `divmod()`: `divmod(x, y) == (x//y, x%y)`.[4]

In addition to performing the modulo operation on numbers, the % operator is also overloaded by string objects to perform old-style string formatting (also known as interpolation). The syntax for string formatting is described in the section *Old String Formatting Operations* in "The Python Library Reference Manual".

The floor division operator, the modulo operator, and the `divmod()` function are not defined for complex numbers. Instead, convert to a floating point number using the `abs()` function if appropriate.

The + (addition) operator yields the sum of its arguments. The arguments must either both be numbers or both sequences of the same type. In the former case, the numbers are converted to a common type and then added together. In the latter case, the sequences are concatenated.

The - (subtraction) operator yields the difference of its arguments. The numeric arguments are first converted to a common type.

5.7. Shifting operations

The shifting operations have lower priority than the arithmetic operations:

```
shift_expr  ::=  a_expr | shift_expr ( "<<" | ">>" ) a_expr
```

These operators accept integers as arguments. They shift the first argument to the left or right by the number of bits given by the second argument.

A right shift by n bits is defined as division by $pow(2,n)$. A left shift by n bits is defined as multiplication with $pow(2,n)$.

Note: In the current implementation, the right-hand operand is required to be at most `sys.maxsize`. If the right-hand operand is larger than `sys.maxsize` an OverflowError exception is raised.

---

[3]While `abs(x%y) < abs(y)` is true mathematically, for floats it may not be true numerically due to roundoff. For example, and assuming a platform on which a Python float is an IEEE 754 double-precision number, in order that `-1e-100 % 1e100` have the same sign as 1e100, the computed result is `-1e-100 + 1e100`, which is numerically exactly equal to 1e100. The function `math.fmod()` returns a result whose sign matches the sign of the first argument instead, and so returns `-1e-100` in this case. Which approach is more appropriate depends on the application.

[4]If x is very close to an exact integer multiple of y, it's possible for `x//y` to be one larger than `(x-x%y)//y` due to rounding. In such cases, Python returns the latter result, in order to preserve that `divmod(x,y)[0] * y + x % y` be very close to x.

5.8. Binary bitwise operations

Each of the three bitwise operations has a different priority level:

```
and_expr  ::=  shift_expr | and_expr "&" shift_expr
xor_expr  ::=  and_expr | xor_expr "^" and_expr
or_expr   ::=  xor_expr | or_expr "|" xor_expr
```

The & operator yields the bitwise AND of its arguments, which must be integers.

The ^ operator yields the bitwise XOR (exclusive OR) of its arguments, which must be integers.

The | operator yields the bitwise (inclusive) OR of its arguments, which must be integers.

5.9. Comparisons

Unlike C, all comparison operations in Python have the same priority, which is lower than that of any arithmetic, shifting or bitwise operation. Also unlike C, expressions like a < b < c have the interpretation that is conventional in mathematics:

```
comparison     ::=  or_expr ( comp_operator or_expr )*
comp_operator  ::=  "<" | ">" | "==" | ">=" | "<=" | "!="
                  | "is" ["not"] | ["not"] "in"
```

Comparisons yield boolean values: True or False.

Comparisons can be chained arbitrarily, e.g., x < y <= z is equivalent to x < y and y <= z, except that y is evaluated only once (but in both cases z is not evaluated at all when x < y is found to be false).

Formally, if a, b, c, ..., y, z are expressions and op1, op2, ..., opN are comparison operators, then a op1 b op2 c ... y opN z is equivalent to a op1 b and b op2 c and ... y opN z, except that each expression is evaluated at most once.

Note that a op1 b op2 c doesn't imply any kind of comparison between a and c, so that, e.g., x < y > z is perfectly legal (though perhaps not pretty).

The operators <, >, ==, >=, <=, and != compare the values of two objects. The objects need not have the same type. If both are numbers, they are converted to a common type. Otherwise, the == and != operators *always* consider objects of different types to be unequal, while the <, >, >= and <= operators raise a TypeError when comparing objects of different types that do not implement these operators for the given pair of types. You can control comparison behavior of objects of non-built-in types by defining rich comparison methods like __gt__(), described in section 3.3.1 *Basic customization* (page 31).

Comparison of objects of the same type depends on the type:

- Numbers are compared arithmetically.

- The values float('NaN') and Decimal('NaN') are special. The are identical to themselves, x is x but are not equal to themselves, x != x. Additionally, comparing any value to a not-a-number value will return False. For example, both 3 < float('NaN') and float('NaN') < 3 will return False.

- Bytes objects are compared lexicographically using the numeric values of their elements.

- Strings are compared lexicographically using the numeric equivalents (the result of the built-in function ord()) of their characters.[5] String and bytes object can't be compared!

- Tuples and lists are compared lexicographically using comparison of corresponding elements. This means that to compare equal, each element must compare equal and the two sequences must be of the same type and have the same length.

  If not equal, the sequences are ordered the same as their first differing elements. For example, [1,2,x] <= [1,2,y] has the same value as x <= y. If the corresponding element does not exist, the shorter sequence is ordered first (for example, [1,2] < [1,2,3]).

- Mappings (dictionaries) compare equal if and only if they have the same (key, value) pairs. Order comparisons ('<', '<=', '>=', '>') raise TypeError.

- Sets and frozensets define comparison operators to mean subset and superset tests. Those relations do not define total orderings (the two sets {1,2} and {2,3} are not equal, nor subsets of one another, nor supersets of one another). Accordingly, sets are not appropriate arguments for functions which depend on total ordering. For example, min(), max(), and sorted() produce undefined results given a list of sets as inputs.

- Most other objects of built-in types compare unequal unless they are the same object; the choice whether one object is considered smaller or larger than another one is made arbitrarily but consistently within one execution of a program.

Comparison of objects of the differing types depends on whether either of the types provide explicit support for the comparison. Most numeric types can be compared with one another, but comparisons of float and Decimal are not supported to avoid the inevitable confusion arising from representation issues such as float('1.1') being inexactly represented and therefore not exactly equal to Decimal('1.1') which is. When cross-type comparison is not supported, the comparison method returns NotImplemented. This can create the

---

[5]While comparisons between strings make sense at the byte level, they may be counterintuitive to users. For example, the strings "\u00C7" and "\u0327\u0043" compare differently, even though they both represent the same unicode character (LATIN CAPITAL LETTER C WITH CEDILLA). To compare strings in a human recognizable way, compare using unicodedata.normalize().

illusion of non-transitivity between supported cross-type comparisons and un-supported comparisons. For example, Decimal(2) == 2 and 2 == float(2) but Decimal(2) != float(2). The operators in and not in test for member-ship. x in s evaluates to true if *x* is a member of *s*, and false otherwise. x not in s returns the negation of x in s. All built-in sequences and set types support this as well as dictionary, for which in tests whether a the dictionary has a given key. For container types such as list, tuple, set, frozenset, dict, or collections.deque, the expression x in y is equivalent to any(x is e or x == e for e in y).

For the string and bytes types, x in y is true if and only if *x* is a substring of *y*. An equivalent test is y.find(x) != -1. Empty strings are always considered to be a substring of any other string, so "" in "abc" will return True.

For user-defined classes which define the __contains__() method, x in y is true if and only if y.__contains__(x) is true.

For user-defined classes which do not define __contains__() but do define __iter__(), x in y is true if some value z with x == z is produced while iter-ating over y. If an exception is raised during the iteration, it is as if in raised that exception.

Lastly, the old-style iteration protocol is tried: if a class defines __getitem__(), x in y is true if and only if there is a non-negative integer index *i* such that x == y[i], and all lower integer indices do not raise IndexError exception. (If any other exception is raised, it is as if in raised that exception.)

The operator not in is defined to have the inverse true value of in.

The operators is and is not test for object identity: x is y is true if and only if *x* and *y* are the same object. x is not y yields the inverse truth value.[6]

5.10. Boolean operations

```
or_test   ::=  and_test | or_test "or" and_test
and_test  ::=  not_test | and_test "and" not_test
not_test  ::=  comparison | "not" not_test
```

In the context of Boolean operations, and also when expressions are used by control flow statements, the following values are interpreted as false: False, None, numeric zero of all types, and empty strings and containers (including strings, tuples, lists, dictionaries, sets and frozensets). All other values are interpreted as true. User-defined objects can customize their truth value by providing a __bool__() method.

The operator not yields True if its argument is false, False otherwise.

[6] Due to automatic garbage-collection, free lists, and the dynamic nature of descriptors, you may notice seemingly unusual behaviour in certain uses of the is operator, like those in-volving comparisons between instance methods, or constants. Check their documentation for more info.

The expression x and y first evaluates x; if x is false, its value is returned; otherwise, y is evaluated and the resulting value is returned.

The expression x or y first evaluates x; if x is true, its value is returned; otherwise, y is evaluated and the resulting value is returned.

(Note that neither and nor or restrict the value and type they return to False and True, but rather return the last evaluated argument. This is sometimes useful, e.g., if s is a string that should be replaced by a default value if it is empty, the expression s or 'foo' yields the desired value. Because not has to invent a value anyway, it does not bother to return a value of the same type as its argument, so e.g., not 'foo' yields False, not ''.)

5.11. Conditional expressions

```
conditional_expression  ::=  or_test ["if" or_test "else"
                                 expression]
expression              ::=  conditional_expression |
                                 lambda_form
expression_nocond       ::=  or_test | lambda_form_nocond
```

Conditional expressions (sometimes called a "ternary operator") have the lowest priority of all Python operations.

The expression x if C else y first evaluates the condition, C (not x); if C is true, x is evaluated and its value is returned; otherwise, y is evaluated and its value is returned.

See **PEP 308**[7] for more details about conditional expressions.

5.12. Lambdas

```
lambda_form             ::=  "lambda" [parameter_list]:
                                 expression
lambda_form_nocond      ::=  "lambda" [parameter_list]:
                                 expression_nocond
```

Lambda forms (lambda expressions) have the same syntactic position as expressions. They are a shorthand to create anonymous functions; the expression lambda arguments: expression yields a function object. The unnamed object behaves like a function object defined with

```
def <lambda>(arguments):
    return expression
```

See section 7.6 *Function definitions* (page 94) for the syntax of parameter lists. Note that functions created with lambda forms cannot contain statements or annotations.

---

[7]http://www.python.org/dev/peps/pep-0308

5.13. Expression lists

```
expression_list  ::=  expression ( "," expression )* [","]
```

An expression list containing at least one comma yields a tuple. The length of the tuple is the number of expressions in the list. The expressions are evaluated from left to right.

The trailing comma is required only to create a single tuple (a.k.a. a *singleton*); it is optional in all other cases. A single expression without a trailing comma doesn't create a tuple, but rather yields the value of that expression. (To create an empty tuple, use an empty pair of parentheses: ().)

5.14. Evaluation order

Python evaluates expressions from left to right. Notice that while evaluating an assignment, the right-hand side is evaluated before the left-hand side.

In the following lines, expressions will be evaluated in the arithmetic order of their suffixes:

```
expr1, expr2, expr3, expr4
(expr1, expr2, expr3, expr4)
{expr1: expr2, expr3: expr4}
expr1 + expr2 * (expr3 - expr4)
expr1(expr2, expr3, *expr4, **expr5)
expr3, expr4 = expr1, expr2
```

5.15. Summary

The following table summarizes the operator precedences in Python, from lowest precedence (least binding) to highest precedence (most binding). Operators in the same box have the same precedence. Unless the syntax is explicitly given, operators are binary. Operators in the same box group left to right (except for comparisons, including tests, which all have the same precedence and chain from left to right — see section 5.9 *Comparisons* (page 66) — and exponentiation, which groups from right to left).

Operator	Description
`lambda`	Lambda expression
`if - else`	Conditional expression
`or`	Boolean OR
`and`	Boolean AND
`not x`	Boolean NOT
`in, not in, is, is not, <, <=, >, >=,` `!=, ==`	Comparisons, including membership tests and identity tests,
`|`	Bitwise OR
`^`	Bitwise XOR
`&`	Bitwise AND
`<<, >>`	Shifts
`+, -`	Addition and subtraction
`*, /, //, %`	Multiplication, division, remainder[8]
`+x, -x, ~x`	Positive, negative, bitwise NOT
`**`	Exponentiation[9]
`x[index]`, `x[index:index]`, `x(arguments...)`, `x.attribute`	Subscription, slicing, call, attribute reference
`(expressions...)`, `[expressions...]`, `{key:datum...}`, `{expressions...}`	Binding or tuple display, list display, dictionary display, set display

---

[8]The `%` operator is also used for string formatting; the same precedence applies.

[9]The power operator `**` binds less tightly than an arithmetic or bitwise unary operator on its right, that is, `2**-1` is `0.5`.

6. Simple statements

Simple statements are comprised within a single logical line. Several simple statements may occur on a single line separated by semicolons. The syntax for simple statements is:

```
simple_stmt  ::=  expression_stmt
                | assert_stmt
                | assignment_stmt
                | augmented_assignment_stmt
                | pass_stmt
                | del_stmt
                | return_stmt
                | yield_stmt
                | raise_stmt
                | break_stmt
                | continue_stmt
                | import_stmt
                | global_stmt
                | nonlocal_stmt
```

6.1. Expression statements

Expression statements are used (mostly interactively) to compute and write a value, or (usually) to call a procedure (a function that returns no meaningful result; in Python, procedures return the value None). Other uses of expression statements are allowed and occasionally useful. The syntax for an expression statement is:

```
expression_stmt  ::=  expression_list
```

An expression statement evaluates the expression list (which may be a single expression).

In interactive mode, if the value is not None, it is converted to a string using the built-in repr() function and the resulting string is written to standard output on a line by itself (except if the result is None, so that procedure calls do not cause any output.)

6.2. Assignment statements

Assignment statements are used to (re)bind names to values and to modify attributes or items of mutable objects:

```
assignment_stmt   ::=  (target_list "=")+ (expression_list |
                       yield_expression)
target_list       ::=  target ("," target)* [","]
target            ::=  identifier
                       | "(" target_list ")"
                       | "[" target_list "]"
                       | attributeref
                       | subscription
                       | slicing
                       | "*" target
```

(See section 5.3 *Primaries*, page 59, for the syntax definitions for the last three symbols.)

An assignment statement evaluates the expression list (remember that this can be a single expression or a comma-separated list, the latter yielding a tuple) and assigns the single resulting object to each of the target lists, from left to right.

Assignment is defined recursively depending on the form of the target (list). When a target is part of a mutable object (an attribute reference, subscription or slicing), the mutable object must ultimately perform the assignment and decide about its validity, and may raise an exception if the assignment is unacceptable. The rules observed by various types and the exceptions raised are given with the definition of the object types (see section 3.2 *The standard type hierarchy*, page 20).

Assignment of an object to a target list, optionally enclosed in parentheses or square brackets, is recursively defined as follows.

- If the target list is a single target: The object is assigned to that target.

- If the target list is a comma-separated list of targets: The object must be an iterable with the same number of items as there are targets in the target list, and the items are assigned, from left to right, to the corresponding targets. (This rule is relaxed as of Python 1.5; in earlier versions, the object had to be a tuple. Since strings are sequences, an assignment like a, b = "xy" is now legal as long as the string has the right length.)

  - If the target list contains one target prefixed with an asterisk, called a "starred" target: The object must be a sequence with at least as many items as there are targets in the target list, minus one. The first items of the sequence are assigned, from left to right, to the targets before the starred target. The final items of the sequence are assigned to the targets after the starred target. A list of the remaining items in the sequence is then assigned to the starred target (the list can be empty).

  - Else: The object must be a sequence with the same number of items as there are targets in the target list, and the items are assigned, from left to right, to the corresponding targets.

Assignment of an object to a single target is recursively defined as follows.

- If the target is an identifier (name):

  - If the name does not occur in a global or nonlocal statement in the current code block: the name is bound to the object in the current local namespace.

  - Otherwise: the name is bound to the object in the global namespace or the outer namespace determined by nonlocal, respectively.

  The name is rebound if it was already bound. This may cause the reference count for the object previously bound to the name to reach zero, causing the object to be deallocated and its destructor (if it has one) to be called.

- If the target is a target list enclosed in parentheses or in square brackets: The object must be an iterable with the same number of items as there are targets in the target list, and its items are assigned, from left to right, to the corresponding targets.

- If the target is an attribute reference: The primary expression in the reference is evaluated. It should yield an object with assignable attributes; if this is not the case, TypeError is raised. That object is then asked to assign the assigned object to the given attribute; if it cannot perform the assignment, it raises an exception (usually but not necessarily AttributeError). Note: If the object is a class instance and the attribute reference occurs on both sides of the assignment operator, the RHS expression, a.x can access either an instance attribute or (if no instance attribute exists) a class attribute. The LHS target a.x is always set as an instance attribute, creating it if necessary. Thus, the two occurrences of a.x do not necessarily refer to the same attribute: if the RHS expression refers to a class attribute, the LHS creates a new instance attribute as the target of the assignment:

  ```
  class Cls:
      x = 3                  # class variable
  inst = Cls()
  inst.x = inst.x + 1    # writes inst.x as 4 leaving Cls.x as 3
  ```

  This description does not necessarily apply to descriptor attributes, such as properties created with property().

- If the target is a subscription: The primary expression in the reference is evaluated. It should yield either a mutable sequence object (such as a list) or a mapping object (such as a dictionary). Next, the subscript expression is evaluated.

  If the primary is a mutable sequence object (such as a list), the subscript must yield an integer. If it is negative, the sequence's length is added to it. The resulting value must be a nonnegative integer less than the sequence's length, and the sequence is asked to assign the assigned object to its item with that index. If the index is out of range, IndexError is raised (assignment to a subscripted sequence cannot add new items to a list).

If the primary is a mapping object (such as a dictionary), the subscript must have a type compatible with the mapping's key type, and the mapping is then asked to create a key/datum pair which maps the subscript to the assigned object. This can either replace an existing key/value pair with the same key value, or insert a new key/value pair (if no key with the same value existed).

For user-defined objects, the __setitem__() method is called with appropriate arguments.

- If the target is a slicing: The primary expression in the reference is evaluated. It should yield a mutable sequence object (such as a list). The assigned object should be a sequence object of the same type. Next, the lower and upper bound expressions are evaluated, insofar they are present; defaults are zero and the sequence's length. The bounds should evaluate to integers. If either bound is negative, the sequence's length is added to it. The resulting bounds are clipped to lie between zero and the sequence's length, inclusive. Finally, the sequence object is asked to replace the slice with the items of the assigned sequence. The length of the slice may be different from the length of the assigned sequence, thus changing the length of the target sequence, if the object allows it.

CPython implementation detail: In the current implementation, the syntax for targets is taken to be the same as for expressions, and invalid syntax is rejected during the code generation phase, causing less detailed error messages.

WARNING: Although the definition of assignment implies that overlaps between the left-hand side and the right-hand side are 'safe' (for example a, b = b, a swaps two variables), overlaps *within* the collection of assigned-to variables are not safe! For instance, the following program prints [0, 2]:

```
x = [0, 1]
i = 0
i, x[i] = 1, 2
print(x)
```

See Also:

PEP 3132[1] **- Extended Iterable Unpacking** The specification for the *target feature.

6.2.1. Augmented assignment statements

Augmented assignment is the combination, in a single statement, of a binary operation and an assignment statement:

---

[1]http://www.python.org/dev/peps/pep-3132

```
augmented_assignment_stmt  ::=  augtarget augop
                                (expression_list |
                                yield_expression)
augtarget                  ::=  identifier | attributeref |
                                subscription | slicing
augop                      ::=  "+=" | "-=" | "*=" | "/=" |
                                "//=" | "%=" | "**="
                                | ">>=" | "<<=" | "&=" | "^="
                                | "|="
```

(See section 5.3 *Primaries*, page 59, for the syntax definitions for the last three symbols.)

An augmented assignment evaluates the target (which, unlike normal assignment statements, cannot be an unpacking) and the expression list, performs the binary operation specific to the type of assignment on the two operands, and assigns the result to the original target. The target is only evaluated once.

An augmented assignment expression like x += 1 can be rewritten as x = x + 1 to achieve a similar, but not exactly equal effect. In the augmented version, x is only evaluated once. Also, when possible, the actual operation is performed *in-place*, meaning that rather than creating a new object and assigning that to the target, the old object is modified instead.

With the exception of assigning to tuples and multiple targets in a single statement, the assignment done by augmented assignment statements is handled the same way as normal assignments. Similarly, with the exception of the possible *in-place* behavior, the binary operation performed by augmented assignment is the same as the normal binary operations.

For targets which are attribute references, the same *caveat about class and instance attributes* (page 75) applies as for regular assignments.

6.3. The assert statement

Assert statements are a convenient way to insert debugging assertions into a program:

```
assert_stmt  ::=  "assert" expression ["," expression]
```

The simple form, assert expression, is equivalent to

```
if __debug__:
    if not expression: raise AssertionError
```

The extended form, assert expression1, expression2, is equivalent to

```
if __debug__:
    if not expression1: raise AssertionError(expression2)
```

These equivalences assume that __debug__ and AssertionError refer to the built-in variables with those names. In the current implementation, the built-in variable __debug__ is True under normal circumstances, False when optimization is requested (command line option -O). The current code generator emits no code for an assert statement when optimization is requested at compile time. Note that it is unnecessary to include the source code for the expression that failed in the error message; it will be displayed as part of the stack trace.

Assignments to __debug__ are illegal. The value for the built-in variable is determined when the interpreter starts.

6.4. The pass statement

```
pass_stmt  ::=  "pass"
```

pass is a null operation — when it is executed, nothing happens. It is useful as a placeholder when a statement is required syntactically, but no code needs to be executed, for example:

```
def f(arg): pass      # a function that does nothing (yet)

class C: pass         # a class with no methods (yet)
```

6.5. The del statement

```
del_stmt  ::=  "del" target_list
```

Deletion is recursively defined very similar to the way assignment is defined. Rather than spelling it out in full details, here are some hints.

Deletion of a target list recursively deletes each target, from left to right.

Deletion of a name removes the binding of that name from the local or global namespace, depending on whether the name occurs in a global statement in the same code block. If the name is unbound, a NameError exception will be raised.

Deletion of attribute references, subscriptions and slicings is passed to the primary object involved; deletion of a slicing is in general equivalent to assignment of an empty slice of the right type (but even this is determined by the sliced object). Changed in version 3.2.

6.6. The return statement

```
return_stmt  ::=  "return" [expression_list]
```

return may only occur syntactically nested in a function definition, not within a nested class definition.

If an expression list is present, it is evaluated, else None is substituted.

return leaves the current function call with the expression list (or None) as return value.

When return passes control out of a try statement with a finally clause, that finally clause is executed before really leaving the function.

In a generator function, the return statement is not allowed to include an expression_list. In that context, a bare return indicates that the generator is done and will cause StopIteration to be raised.

6.7. The yield statement

```
yield_stmt  ::=  yield_expression
```

The yield statement is only used when defining a generator function, and is only used in the body of the generator function. Using a yield statement in a function definition is sufficient to cause that definition to create a generator function instead of a normal function. When a generator function is called, it returns an iterator known as a generator iterator, or more commonly, a generator. The body of the generator function is executed by calling the next() function on the generator repeatedly until it raises an exception.

When a yield statement is executed, the state of the generator is frozen and the value of expression_list is returned to next()'s caller. By "frozen" we mean that all local state is retained, including the current bindings of local variables, the instruction pointer, and the internal evaluation stack: enough information is saved so that the next time next() is invoked, the function can proceed exactly as if the yield statement were just another external call.

The yield statement is allowed in the try clause of a try ... finally construct. If the generator is not resumed before it is finalized (by reaching a zero reference count or by being garbage collected), the generator-iterator's close() method will be called, allowing any pending finally clauses to execute.

See Also:

PEP 0255[2] - Simple Generators The proposal for adding generators and the yield statement to Python.

PEP 0342[3] - Coroutines via Enhanced Generators The proposal that, among other generator enhancements, proposed allowing yield to appear inside a try ... finally block.

6.8. The raise statement

```
raise_stmt  ::=  "raise" [expression ["from" expression]]
```

If no expressions are present, raise re-raises the last exception that was active in the current scope. If no exception is active in the current scope, a TypeError exception is raised indicating that this is an error (if running under IDLE, a queue.Empty exception is raised instead).

---

[2]http://www.python.org/dev/peps/pep-0255
[3]http://www.python.org/dev/peps/pep-0342

Otherwise, raise evaluates the first expression as the exception object. It must be either a subclass or an instance of BaseException. If it is a class, the exception instance will be obtained when needed by instantiating the class with no arguments.

The *type* of the exception is the exception instance's class, the *value* is the instance itself.

A traceback object is normally created automatically when an exception is raised and attached to it as the __traceback__ attribute, which is writable. You can create an exception and set your own traceback in one step using the with_traceback() exception method (which returns the same exception instance, with its traceback set to its argument), like so:

```
raise Exception("foo occurred").with_traceback(tracebackobj)
```

The from clause is used for exception chaining: if given, the second *expression* must be another exception class or instance, which will then be attached to the raised exception as the __cause__ attribute (which is writable). If the raised exception is not handled, both exceptions will be printed:

```
>>> try:
...     print(1 / 0)
... except Exception as exc:
...     raise RuntimeError("Something bad happened") from exc...

Traceback (most recent call last):
  File "<stdin>", line 2, in <module>
ZeroDivisionError: int division or modulo by zero

The above exception was the direct cause of the following exception:

Traceback (most recent call last):
  File "<stdin>", line 4, in <module>
RuntimeError: Something bad happened
```

A similar mechanism works implicitly if an exception is raised inside an exception handler: the previous exception is then attached as the new exception's __context__ attribute:

```
>>> try:
...     print(1 / 0)
... except:
...     raise RuntimeError("Something bad happened")
...
Traceback (most recent call last):
  File "<stdin>", line 2, in <module>
ZeroDivisionError: int division or modulo by zero

During handling of the above exception, another exception occurred:
```

```
Traceback (most recent call last):
  File "<stdin>", line 4, in <module>
RuntimeError: Something bad happened
```

Additional information on exceptions can be found in section 4.2 *Exceptions* (page 51), and information about handling exceptions is in section 7.4 *The try statement* (page 91).

6.9. The break statement

```
break_stmt   ::=   "break"
```

break may only occur syntactically nested in a for or while loop, but not nested in a function or class definition within that loop.

It terminates the nearest enclosing loop, skipping the optional else clause if the loop has one.

If a for loop is terminated by break, the loop control target keeps its current value.

When break passes control out of a try statement with a finally clause, that finally clause is executed before really leaving the loop.

6.10. The continue statement

```
continue_stmt   ::=   "continue"
```

continue may only occur syntactically nested in a for or while loop, but not nested in a function or class definition or finally clause within that loop. It continues with the next cycle of the nearest enclosing loop.

When continue passes control out of a try statement with a finally clause, that finally clause is executed before really starting the next loop cycle.

6.11. The import statement

```
import_stmt       ::=   "import" module ["as" name] ( ","
                        module ["as" name] )*
                        | "from" relative_module "import"
                        identifier ["as" name]
                        ( "," identifier ["as" name] )*
                        | "from" relative_module "import" "("
                        identifier ["as" name]
                        ( "," identifier ["as" name] )* [","]
                        ")"
                        | "from" module "import" "*"
module            ::=   (identifier ".")* identifier
relative_module   ::=   "."* module | "."+
name              ::=   identifier
```

Import statements are executed in two steps: (1) find a module, and initialize it if necessary; (2) define a name or names in the local namespace (of the scope where the import statement occurs). The statement comes in two forms differing on whether it uses the from keyword. The first form (without from) repeats these steps for each identifier in the list. The form with from performs step (1) once, and then performs step (2) repeatedly. For a reference implementation of step (1), see the importlib module.

To understand how step (1) occurs, one must first understand how Python handles hierarchical naming of modules. To help organize modules and provide a hierarchy in naming, Python has a concept of packages. A package can contain other packages and modules while modules cannot contain other modules or packages. From a file system perspective, packages are directories and modules are files. The original specification for packages[4] is still available to read, although minor details have changed since the writing of that document.

Once the name of the module is known (unless otherwise specified, the term "module" will refer to both packages and modules), searching for the module or package can begin. The first place checked is sys.modules, the cache of all modules that have been imported previously. If the module is found there then it is used in step (2) of import unless None is found in sys.modules, in which case ImportError is raised.

If the module is not found in the cache, then sys.meta_path is searched (the specification for sys.meta_path can be found in **PEP 302**[5]). The object is a list of *finder* objects which are queried in order as to whether they know how to load the module by calling their find_module() method with the name of the module. If the module happens to be contained within a package (as denoted by the existence of a dot in the name), then a second argument to find_module() is given as the value of the __path__ attribute from the parent package (everything up to the last dot in the name of the module being imported). If a finder can find the module it returns a *loader* (discussed later) or returns None.

If none of the finders on sys.meta_path are able to find the module then some implicitly defined finders are queried. Implementations of Python vary in what implicit meta path finders are defined. The one they all do define, though, is one that handles sys.path_hooks, sys.path_importer_cache, and sys.path.

The implicit finder searches for the requested module in the "paths" specified in one of two places ("paths" do not have to be file system paths). If the module being imported is supposed to be contained within a package then the second argument passed to find_module(), __path__ on the parent package, is used as the source of paths. If the module is not contained in a package then sys.path is used as the source of paths.

Once the source of paths is chosen it is iterated over to find a finder that can handle that path. The dict at sys.path_importer_cache caches finders for

---

[4]http://www.python.org/doc/essays/packages.html
[5]http://www.python.org/dev/peps/pep-0302

paths and is checked for a finder. If the path does not have a finder cached then sys.path_hooks is searched by calling each object in the list with a single argument of the path, returning a finder or raises ImportError. If a finder is returned then it is cached in sys.path_importer_cache and then used for that path entry. If no finder can be found but the path exists then a value of None is stored in sys.path_importer_cache to signify that an implicit, file-based finder that handles modules stored as individual files should be used for that path. If the path does not exist then a finder which always returns None is placed in the cache for the path.

If no finder can find the module then ImportError is raised. Otherwise some finder returned a loader whose load_module() method is called with the name of the module to load (see **PEP 302**[6] for the original definition of loaders). A loader has several responsibilities to perform on a module it loads. First, if the module already exists in sys.modules (a possibility if the loader is called outside of the import machinery) then it is to use that module for initialization and not a new module. But if the module does not exist in sys.modules then it is to be added to that dict before initialization begins. If an error occurs during loading of the module and it was added to sys.modules it is to be removed from the dict. If an error occurs but the module was already in sys.modules it is left in the dict.

The loader must set several attributes on the module. __name__ is to be set to the name of the module. __file__ is to be the "path" to the file unless the module is built-in (and thus listed in sys.builtin_module_names) in which case the attribute is not set. If what is being imported is a package then __path__ is to be set to a list of paths to be searched when looking for modules and packages contained within the package being imported. __package__ is optional but should be set to the name of package that contains the module or package (the empty string is used for module not contained in a package). __loader__ is also optional but should be set to the loader object that is loading the module.

If an error occurs during loading then the loader raises ImportError if some other exception is not already being propagated. Otherwise the loader returns the module that was loaded and initialized.

When step (1) finishes without raising an exception, step (2) can begin.

The first form of import statement binds the module name in the local namespace to the module object, and then goes on to import the next identifier, if any. If the module name is followed by as, the name following as is used as the local name for the module.

The from form does not bind the module name: it goes through the list of identifiers, looks each one of them up in the module found in step (1), and binds the name in the local namespace to the object thus found. As with the first form of import, an alternate local name can be supplied by specifying "as localname". If a name is not found, ImportError is raised. If the list of

---

[6]http://www.python.org/dev/peps/pep-0302

identifiers is replaced by a star ('*'), all public names defined in the module are bound in the local namespace of the import statement.

The *public names* defined by a module are determined by checking the module's namespace for a variable named __all__; if defined, it must be a sequence of strings which are names defined or imported by that module. The names given in __all__ are all considered public and are required to exist. If __all__ is not defined, the set of public names includes all names found in the module's namespace which do not begin with an underscore character ('_'). __all__ should contain the entire public API. It is intended to avoid accidentally exporting items that are not part of the API (such as library modules which were imported and used within the module).

The from form with * may only occur in a module scope. The wild card form of import — import * — is only allowed at the module level. Attempting to use it in class or function definitions will raise a SyntaxError.

When specifying what module to import you do not have to specify the absolute name of the module. When a module or package is contained within another package it is possible to make a relative import within the same top package without having to mention the package name. By using leading dots in the specified module or package after from you can specify how high to traverse up the current package hierarchy without specifying exact names. One leading dot means the current package where the module making the import exists. Two dots means up one package level. Three dots is up two levels, etc. So if you execute from . import mod from a module in the pkg package then you will end up importing pkg.mod. If you execute from ..subpkg2 import mod from within pkg.subpkg1 you will import pkg.subpkg2.mod. The specification for relative imports is contained within **PEP 328**[7].

importlib.import_module() is provided to support applications that determine which modules need to be loaded dynamically.

6.11.1. Future statements

A *future statement* is a directive to the compiler that a particular module should be compiled using syntax or semantics that will be available in a specified future release of Python. The future statement is intended to ease migration to future versions of Python that introduce incompatible changes to the language. It allows use of the new features on a per-module basis before the release in which the feature becomes standard.

---

[7]http://www.python.org/dev/peps/pep-0328

```
future_statement    ::=   "from" "__future__" "import" feature
                          ["as" name]
                          ("," feature ["as" name])*
                          | "from" "__future__" "import" "("
                          feature ["as" name]
                          ("," feature ["as" name])* [","] ")"
feature             ::=   identifier
name                ::=   identifier
```

A future statement must appear near the top of the module. The only lines
that can appear before a future statement are:

- the module docstring (if any),

- comments,

- blank lines, and

- other future statements.

The features recognized by Python 3.0 are absolute_import, division,
generators, unicode_literals, print_function, nested_scopes and
with_statement. They are all redundant because they are always enabled, and
only kept for backwards compatibility.

A future statement is recognized and treated specially at compile time: Changes
to the semantics of core constructs are often implemented by generating different
code. It may even be the case that a new feature introduces new incompatible
syntax (such as a new reserved word), in which case the compiler may need to
parse the module differently. Such decisions cannot be pushed off until runtime.

For any given release, the compiler knows which feature names have been defined, and raises a compile-time error if a future statement contains a feature
not known to it.

The direct runtime semantics are the same as for any import statement: there
is a standard module __future__, described later, and it will be imported in
the usual way at the time the future statement is executed.

The interesting runtime semantics depend on the specific feature enabled by the
future statement.

Note that there is nothing special about the statement:

```
import __future__ [as name]
```

That is not a future statement; it's an ordinary import statement with no special
semantics or syntax restrictions.

Code compiled by calls to the built-in functions exec() and compile() that
occur in a module M containing a future statement will, by default, use the
new syntax or semantics associated with the future statement. This can be
controlled by optional arguments to compile() — see the documentation of
that function for details.

A future statement typed at an interactive interpreter prompt will take effect for the rest of the interpreter session. If an interpreter is started with the -*i* option, is passed a script name to execute, and the script includes a future statement, it will be in effect in the interactive session started after the script is executed.

See Also:

> **PEP 236**[8] **- Back to the __future__** The original proposal for the __future__ mechanism.

6.12. The global statement

```
global_stmt  ::=  "global" identifier ("," identifier)*
```

The global statement is a declaration which holds for the entire current code block. It means that the listed identifiers are to be interpreted as globals. It would be impossible to assign to a global variable without global, although free variables may refer to globals without being declared global.

Names listed in a global statement must not be used in the same code block textually preceding that global statement.

Names listed in a global statement must not be defined as formal parameters or in a for loop control target, class definition, function definition, or import statement.

CPython implementation detail: The current implementation does not enforce the latter two restrictions, but programs should not abuse this freedom, as future implementations may enforce them or silently change the meaning of the program.

Programmer's note: the global is a directive to the parser. It applies only to code parsed at the same time as the global statement. In particular, a global statement contained in a string or code object supplied to the built-in exec() function does not affect the code block *containing* the function call, and code contained in such a string is unaffected by global statements in the code containing the function call. The same applies to the eval() and compile() functions.

6.13. The nonlocal statement

```
nonlocal_stmt  ::=  "nonlocal" identifier ("," identifier)*
```

The nonlocal statement causes the listed identifiers to refer to previously bound variables in the nearest enclosing scope. This is important because the default behavior for binding is to search the local namespace first. The statement allows encapsulated code to rebind variables outside of the local scope besides the global (module) scope.

---

[8]http://www.python.org/dev/peps/pep-0236

Names listed in a `nonlocal` statement, unlike to those listed in a `global` statement, must refer to pre-existing bindings in an enclosing scope (the scope in which a new binding should be created cannot be determined unambiguously).

Names listed in a `nonlocal` statement must not collide with pre-existing bindings in the local scope.

See Also:

PEP 3104[9] - Access to Names in Outer Scopes The specification for the `nonlocal` statement.

---

[9] http://www.python.org/dev/peps/pep-3104

7. Compound statements

Compound statements contain (groups of) other statements; they affect or control the execution of those other statements in some way. In general, compound statements span multiple lines, although in simple incarnations a whole compound statement may be contained in one line.

The if, while and for statements implement traditional control flow constructs. try specifies exception handlers and/or cleanup code for a group of statements, while the with statement allows the execution of initialization and finalization code around a block of code. Function and class definitions are also syntactically compound statements.

Compound statements consist of one or more 'clauses.' A clause consists of a header and a 'suite.' The clause headers of a particular compound statement are all at the same indentation level. Each clause header begins with a uniquely identifying keyword and ends with a colon. A suite is a group of statements controlled by a clause. A suite can be one or more semicolon-separated simple statements on the same line as the header, following the header's colon, or it can be one or more indented statements on subsequent lines. Only the latter form of suite can contain nested compound statements; the following is illegal, mostly because it wouldn't be clear to which if clause a following else clause would belong:

```
if test1: if test2: print(x)
```

Also note that the semicolon binds tighter than the colon in this context, so that in the following example, either all or none of the print() calls are executed:

```
if x < y < z: print(x); print(y); print(z)
```

Summarizing:

```
compound_stmt  ::=  if_stmt
                    | while_stmt
                    | for_stmt
                    | try_stmt
                    | with_stmt
                    | funcdef
                    | classdef
suite          ::=  stmt_list NEWLINE | NEWLINE INDENT
                    statement+ DEDENT
statement      ::=  stmt_list NEWLINE | compound_stmt
stmt_list      ::=  simple_stmt (";" simple_stmt)* [";"]
```

Note that statements always end in a NEWLINE possibly followed by a DEDENT. Also note that optional continuation clauses always begin with a keyword that cannot start a statement, thus there are no ambiguities (the 'dangling else' problem is solved in Python by requiring nested if statements to be indented).

The formatting of the grammar rules in the following sections places each clause on a separate line for clarity.

7.1. The if statement

The if statement is used for conditional execution:

```
if_stmt  ::=  "if" expression ":" suite
              ( "elif" expression ":" suite )*
              ["else" ":" suite]
```

It selects exactly one of the suites by evaluating the expressions one by one until one is found to be true (see section 5.10 *Boolean operations*, page 68, for the definition of true and false); then that suite is executed (and no other part of the if statement is executed or evaluated). If all expressions are false, the suite of the else clause, if present, is executed.

7.2. The while statement

The while statement is used for repeated execution as long as an expression is true:

```
while_stmt  ::=  "while" expression ":" suite
                 ["else" ":" suite]
```

This repeatedly tests the expression and, if it is true, executes the first suite; if the expression is false (which may be the first time it is tested) the suite of the else clause, if present, is executed and the loop terminates.

A break statement executed in the first suite terminates the loop without executing the else clause's suite. A continue statement executed in the first suite skips the rest of the suite and goes back to testing the expression.

7.3. The for statement

The for statement is used to iterate over the elements of a sequence (such as a string, tuple or list) or other iterable object:

```
for_stmt  ::=  "for" target_list "in" expression_list ":"
               suite
               ["else" ":" suite]
```

The expression list is evaluated once; it should yield an iterable object. An iterator is created for the result of the expression_list. The suite is then executed once for each item provided by the iterator, in the order of ascending indices. Each item in turn is assigned to the target list using the standard rules for assignments (see 6.2 *Assignment statements*, page 73), and then the suite is executed. When the items are exhausted (which is immediately when the sequence is empty or an iterator raises a StopIteration exception), the suite in the else clause, if present, is executed, and the loop terminates.

A break statement executed in the first suite terminates the loop without executing the else clause's suite. A continue statement executed in the first suite skips the rest of the suite and continues with the next item, or with the else clause if there was no next item.

The suite may assign to the variable(s) in the target list; this does not affect the next item assigned to it.

Names in the target list are not deleted when the loop is finished, but if the sequence is empty, it will not have been assigned to at all by the loop. Hint: the built-in function range() returns an iterator of integers suitable to emulate the effect of Pascal's for i := a to b do; e.g., list(range(3)) returns the list [0, 1, 2].

Note: There is a subtlety when the sequence is being modified by the loop (this can only occur for mutable sequences, i.e. lists). An internal counter is used to keep track of which item is used next, and this is incremented on each iteration. When this counter has reached the length of the sequence the loop terminates. This means that if the suite deletes the current (or a previous) item from the sequence, the next item will be skipped (since it gets the index of the current item which has already been treated). Likewise, if the suite inserts an item in the sequence before the current item, the current item will be treated again the next time through the loop. This can lead to nasty bugs that can be avoided by making a temporary copy using a slice of the whole sequence, e.g.,

```
for x in a[:]:
    if x < 0: a.remove(x)
```

7.4. The try statement

The try statement specifies exception handlers and/or cleanup code for a group of statements:

```
try_stmt    ::=  try1_stmt | try2_stmt
try1_stmt   ::=  "try" ":" suite
                 ("except" [expression ["as" target]] ":"
                 suite)+
                 ["else" ":" suite]
                 ["finally" ":" suite]
try2_stmt   ::=  "try" ":" suite
                 "finally" ":" suite
```

The except clause(s) specify one or more exception handlers. When no exception occurs in the try clause, no exception handler is executed. When an exception occurs in the try suite, a search for an exception handler is started. This search inspects the except clauses in turn until one is found that matches the exception. An expression-less except clause, if present, must be last; it matches any exception. For an except clause with an expression, that expression is evaluated, and the clause matches the exception if the resulting object is "compatible" with the exception. An object is compatible with an exception if it is the class or a base class of the exception object or a tuple containing an item compatible with the exception.

If no except clause matches the exception, the search for an exception handler continues in the surrounding code and on the invocation stack.[1]

If the evaluation of an expression in the header of an except clause raises an exception, the original search for a handler is canceled and a search starts for the new exception in the surrounding code and on the call stack (it is treated as if the entire try statement raised the exception).

When a matching except clause is found, the exception is assigned to the target specified after the as keyword in that except clause, if present, and the except clause's suite is executed. All except clauses must have an executable block. When the end of this block is reached, execution continues normally after the entire try statement. (This means that if two nested handlers exist for the same exception, and the exception occurs in the try clause of the inner handler, the outer handler will not handle the exception.)

When an exception has been assigned using as target, it is cleared at the end of the except clause. This is as if

```
except E as N:
    foo
```

was translated to

```
except E as N:
    try:
        foo
    finally:
        del N
```

This means the exception must be assigned to a different name to be able to refer to it after the except clause. Exceptions are cleared because with the traceback attached to them, they form a reference cycle with the stack frame, keeping all locals in that frame alive until the next garbage collection occurs.

Before an except clause's suite is executed, details about the exception are stored in the sys module and can be access via sys.exc_info(). sys.exc_info() returns a 3-tuple consisting of the exception class, the exception instance and a traceback object (see section 3.2 *The standard type hierarchy*, page 20) identifying the point in the program where the exception occurred. sys.exc_info() values are restored to their previous values (before the call) when returning from a function that handled an exception.

---

[1] The exception is propagated to the invocation stack only if there is no finally clause that negates the exception.

The optional else clause is executed if and when control flows off the end of the try clause.[2] Exceptions in the else clause are not handled by the preceding except clauses.

If finally is present, it specifies a 'cleanup' handler. The try clause is executed, including any except and else clauses. If an exception occurs in any of the clauses and is not handled, the exception is temporarily saved. The finally clause is executed. If there is a saved exception, it is re-raised at the end of the finally clause. If the finally clause raises another exception or executes a return or break statement, the saved exception is lost. The exception information is not available to the program during execution of the finally clause.

When a return, break or continue statement is executed in the try suite of a try...finally statement, the finally clause is also executed 'on the way out.' A continue statement is illegal in the finally clause. (The reason is a problem with the current implementation — this restriction may be lifted in the future).

Additional information on exceptions can be found in section 4.2 *Exceptions* (page 51), and information on using the raise statement to generate exceptions may be found in section 6.8 *The raise statement* (page 79).

7.5. The with statement

The with statement is used to wrap the execution of a block with methods defined by a context manager (see section 3.3.8 *With Statement Context Managers*, page 45). This allows common try...except...finally usage patterns to be encapsulated for convenient reuse.

```
with_stmt  ::=  "with" with_item ("," with_item)* ":" suite
with_item  ::=  expression ["as" target]
```

The execution of the with statement with one "item" proceeds as follows:

1. The context expression (the expression given in the with_item) is evaluated to obtain a context manager.

2. The context manager's __exit__() is loaded for later use.

3. The context manager's __enter__() method is invoked.

4. If a target was included in the with statement, the return value from __enter__() is assigned to it.

   Note: The with statement guarantees that if the __enter__() method returns without an error, then __exit__() will always be called. Thus, if an error occurs during the assignment to the target list, it will be treated the same as an error occurring within the suite would be. See step 6 below.

---

[2]Currently, control "flows off the end" except in the case of an exception or the execution of a return, continue, or break statement.

5. The suite is executed.

6. The context manager's __exit__() method is invoked. If an exception caused the suite to be exited, its type, value, and traceback are passed as arguments to __exit__(). Otherwise, three None arguments are supplied.

   If the suite was exited due to an exception, and the return value from the __exit__() method was false, the exception is reraised. If the return value was true, the exception is suppressed, and execution continues with the statement following the with statement.

   If the suite was exited for any reason other than an exception, the return value from __exit__() is ignored, and execution proceeds at the normal location for the kind of exit that was taken.

With more than one item, the context managers are processed as if multiple with statements were nested:

```
with A() as a, B() as b:
    suite
```

is equivalent to

```
with A() as a:
    with B() as b:
        suite
```

Changed in version 3.1: Support for multiple context expressions.

See Also:

PEP 0343[3] **- The "with" statement** The specification, background, and examples for the Python with statement.

7.6. Function definitions

A function definition defines a user-defined function object (see section 3.2 *The standard type hierarchy*, page 20):

---

[3]http://www.python.org/dev/peps/pep-0343

```
funcdef          ::=  [decorators] "def" funcname "("
                      [parameter_list] ")" ["->" expression]
                      ":" suite
decorators       ::=  decorator+
decorator        ::=  "@" dotted_name ["(" [argument_list
                      [","]] ")"] NEWLINE
dotted_name      ::=  identifier ("." identifier)*
parameter_list   ::=  (defparameter ",")*
                      ( "*" [parameter] ("," defparameter)*
                      [, "**" parameter]
                      | "**" parameter
                      | defparameter [","] )
parameter        ::=  identifier [":" expression]
defparameter     ::=  parameter ["=" expression]
funcname         ::=  identifier
```

A function definition is an executable statement. Its execution binds the function name in the current local namespace to a function object (a wrapper around the executable code for the function). This function object contains a reference to the current global namespace as the global namespace to be used when the function is called.

The function definition does not execute the function body; this gets executed only when the function is called.[4]

A function definition may be wrapped by one or more *decorator* expressions. Decorator expressions are evaluated when the function is defined, in the scope that contains the function definition. The result must be a callable, which is invoked with the function object as the only argument. The returned value is bound to the function name instead of the function object. Multiple decorators are applied in nested fashion. For example, the following code

```
@f1(arg)
@f2
def func(): pass
```

is equivalent to

```
def func(): pass
func = f1(arg)(f2(func))
```

When one or more parameters have the form *parameter* = *expression*, the function is said to have "default parameter values." For a parameter with a default value, the corresponding argument may be omitted from a call, in which case the parameter's default value is substituted. If a parameter has a default value, all following parameters up until the "*" must also have a default value — this is a syntactic restriction that is not expressed by the grammar.

---

[4]A string literal appearing as the first statement in the function body is transformed into the function's __doc__ attribute and therefore the function's *docstring*.

Default parameter values are evaluated when the function definition is executed. This means that the expression is evaluated once, when the function is defined, and that that same "pre-computed" value is used for each call. This is especially important to understand when a default parameter is a mutable object, such as a list or a dictionary: if the function modifies the object (e.g. by appending an item to a list), the default value is in effect modified. This is generally not what was intended. A way around this is to use None as the default, and explicitly test for it in the body of the function, e.g.:

```
def whats_on_the_telly(penguin=None):
    if penguin is None:
        penguin = []
    penguin.append("property of the zoo")
    return penguin
```

Function call semantics are described in more detail in section 5.3.4 *Calls* (page 61). A function call always assigns values to all parameters mentioned in the parameter list, either from position arguments, from keyword arguments, or from default values. If the form "*identifier" is present, it is initialized to a tuple receiving any excess positional parameters, defaulting to the empty tuple. If the form "**identifier" is present, it is initialized to a new dictionary receiving any excess keyword arguments, defaulting to a new empty dictionary. Parameters after "*" or "*identifier" are keyword-only parameters and may only be passed used keyword arguments.

Parameters may have annotations of the form ": expression" following the parameter name. Any parameter may have an annotation even those of the form *identifier or **identifier. Functions may have "return" annotation of the form "-> expression" after the parameter list. These annotations can be any valid Python expression and are evaluated when the function definition is executed. Annotations may be evaluated in a different order than they appear in the source code. The presence of annotations does not change the semantics of a function. The annotation values are available as values of a dictionary keyed by the parameters' names in the __annotations__ attribute of the function object.

It is also possible to create anonymous functions (functions not bound to a name), for immediate use in expressions. This uses lambda forms, described in section 5.12 *Lambdas* (page 69). Note that the lambda form is merely a shorthand for a simplified function definition; a function defined in a "def" statement can be passed around or assigned to another name just like a function defined by a lambda form. The "def" form is actually more powerful since it allows the execution of multiple statements and annotations.

Programmer's note: Functions are first-class objects. A "def" form executed inside a function definition defines a local function that can be returned or passed around. Free variables used in the nested function can access the local variables of the function containing the def. See section 4.1 *Naming and binding* (page 49) for details.

7.7. Class definitions

A class definition defines a class object (see section 3.2 *The standard type hierarchy*, page 20):

```
classdef      ::=  [decorators] "class" classname
                   [inheritance] ":" suite
inheritance   ::=  "(" [argument_list [","] | comprehension]
                   ")"
classname     ::=  identifier
```

A class definition is an executable statement. The inheritance list usually gives a list of base classes (see 3.3.3 *Customizing class creation*, page 39, for more advanced uses), so each item in the list should evaluate to a class object which allows subclassing. Classes without an inheritance list inherit, by default, from the base class object; hence,

```
class Foo:
    pass
```

is equivalent to

```
class Foo(object):
    pass
```

The class's suite is then executed in a new execution frame (see 4.1 *Naming and binding*, page 49), using a newly created local namespace and the original global namespace. (Usually, the suite contains mostly function definitions.) When the class's suite finishes execution, its execution frame is discarded but its local namespace is saved.[5] A class object is then created using the inheritance list for the base classes and the saved local namespace for the attribute dictionary. The class name is bound to this class object in the original local namespace.

Class creation can be customized heavily using 3.3.3 *metaclasses* (page 39).

Classes can also be decorated: just like when decorating functions,

```
@f1(arg)
@f2
class Foo: pass
```

is equivalent to

```
class Foo: pass
Foo = f1(arg)(f2(Foo))
```

The evaluation rules for the decorator expressions are the same as for function decorators. The result must be a class object, which is then bound to the class name.

---

[5] A string literal appearing as the first statement in the class body is transformed into the namespace's __doc__ item and therefore the class's *docstring*.

Programmer's note: Variables defined in the class definition are class attributes; they are shared by instances. Instance attributes can be set in a method with self.name = value. Both class and instance attributes are accessible through the notation "self.name", and an instance attribute hides a class attribute with the same name when accessed in this way. Class attributes can be used as defaults for instance attributes, but using mutable values there can lead to unexpected results. *Descriptors* (page 36) can be used to create instance variables with different implementation details.

See Also:

PEP 3116[6] - Metaclasses in Python 3

PEP 3129[7] - Class Decorators

---

[6]http://www.python.org/dev/peps/pep-3116
[7]http://www.python.org/dev/peps/pep-3129

8. Top-level components

The Python interpreter can get its input from a number of sources: from a script passed to it as standard input or as program argument, typed in interactively, from a module source file, etc. This chapter gives the syntax used in these cases.

8.1. Complete Python programs

While a language specification need not prescribe how the language interpreter is invoked, it is useful to have a notion of a complete Python program. A complete Python program is executed in a minimally initialized environment: all built-in and standard modules are available, but none have been initialized, except for sys (various system services), builtins (built-in functions, exceptions and None) and __main__. The latter is used to provide the local and global namespace for execution of the complete program.

The syntax for a complete Python program is that for file input, described in the next section.

The interpreter may also be invoked in interactive mode; in this case, it does not read and execute a complete program but reads and executes one statement (possibly compound) at a time. The initial environment is identical to that of a complete program; each statement is executed in the namespace of __main__.

Under Unix, a complete program can be passed to the interpreter in three forms: with the -c *string* command line option, as a file passed as the first command line argument, or as standard input. If the file or standard input is a tty device, the interpreter enters interactive mode; otherwise, it executes the file as a complete program.

8.2. File input

All input read from non-interactive files has the same form:

    file_input ::= (NEWLINE | statement)*

This syntax is used in the following situations:

- when parsing a complete Python program (from a file or from a string);
- when parsing a module;
- when parsing a string passed to the exec() function;

8.3. Interactive input

Input in interactive mode is parsed using the following grammar:

```
interactive_input  ::=  [stmt_list] NEWLINE | compound_stmt
                        NEWLINE
```

Note that a (top-level) compound statement must be followed by a blank line in interactive mode; this is needed to help the parser detect the end of the input.

8.4. Expression input

There are two forms of expression input. Both ignore leading whitespace. The string argument to eval() must have the following form:

```
eval_input  ::=  expression_list NEWLINE*
```

Note: to read 'raw' input line without interpretation, you can use the the readline() method of file objects, including sys.stdin.

9. Full Grammar specification

This is the full Python grammar, as it is read by the parser generator and used to parse Python source files:

```
# Grammar for Python

# Note:  Changing the grammar specified in this file will most
#        likely require corresponding changes in the parser
#        module (../Modules/parsermodule.c). If you can't make
#        the changes to that module yourself, please
#        co-ordinate the required changes with someone who can;
#        ask around on python-dev for help. Fred Drake
#        <fdrake@acm.org> will probably be listening there.

# NOTE WELL: You should also follow all the steps listed in PEP
# 306, "How to Change Python's Grammar"

# Start symbols for the grammar:
#        single_input is a single interactive statement;
#        file_input is a module or sequence of commands read
#        from an input file;
#        eval_input is the input for the eval() and input()
#        functions.
# NB: compound_stmt in single_input is followed by extra
# NEWLINE!

single_input:       NEWLINE | simple_stmt | compound_stmt
                    NEWLINE
file_input:         (NEWLINE | stmt)* ENDMARKER
eval_input:         testlist NEWLINE* ENDMARKER

decorator:          '@' dotted_name [ '(' [arglist] ')' ]
                    NEWLINE
decorators:         decorator+
decorated:          decorators (classdef | funcdef)
funcdef:            'def' NAME parameters ['->' test] ':'
                    suite
parameters:         '(' [typedargslist] ')'
```

```
typedargslist:          (tfpdef ['=' test] (',' tfpdef ['='
                        test])* [',' ['*' [tfpdef] (',' tfpdef
                        ['=' test])* [',' '**' tfpdef] | '**'
                        tfpdef]] | '*' [tfpdef] (',' tfpdef
                        ['=' test])* [',' '**' tfpdef] | '**'
                        tfpdef)
tfpdef:                 NAME [':' test]
varargslist:            (vfpdef ['=' test] (',' vfpdef ['='
                        test])* [',' ['*' [vfpdef] (',' vfpdef
                        ['=' test])* [',' '**' vfpdef] | '**'
                        vfpdef]] | '*' [vfpdef] (',' vfpdef
                        ['=' test])* [',' '**' vfpdef] | '**'
                        vfpdef)
vfpdef:                 NAME

stmt:                   simple_stmt | compound_stmt
simple_stmt:            small_stmt (';' small_stmt)* [';']
                        NEWLINE
small_stmt:             (expr_stmt | del_stmt | pass_stmt |
                        flow_stmt | import_stmt | global_stmt
                        | nonlocal_stmt | assert_stmt)
expr_stmt:              testlist_star_expr (augassign
                        (yield_expr|testlist) | ('='
                        (yield_expr|testlist_star_expr))*)
testlist_star_expr:     (test|star_expr) (','
                        (test|star_expr))* [',']
augassign:              ('+=' | '-=' | '*=' | '/=' | '%=' |
                        '&=' | '|=' | '^=' | '<<=' | '>>=' |
                        '**=' | '//=')

# For normal assignments, additional restrictions enforced
# by the interpreter

del_stmt:               'del' exprlist
pass_stmt:              'pass'
flow_stmt:              break_stmt | continue_stmt |
                        return_stmt | raise_stmt | yield_stmt
break_stmt:             'break'
continue_stmt:          'continue'
return_stmt:            'return' [testlist]
yield_stmt:             yield_expr
raise_stmt:             'raise' [test ['from' test]]
import_stmt:            import_name | import_from
import_name:            'import' dotted_as_names
```

```
# note below: the ('.' | '...') is necessary because '...'
# is tokenized as ELLIPSIS

import_from:            ('from' (('.' | '...')* dotted_name
                        | ('.' | '...')+) 'import' ('*'
                        | '(' import_as_names ')' |
                        import_as_names))
import_as_name:         NAME ['as' NAME]
dotted_as_name:         dotted_name ['as' NAME]
import_as_names:        import_as_name (',' import_as_name)*
                        [',']
dotted_as_names:        dotted_as_name (',' dotted_as_name)*
dotted_name:            NAME ('.' NAME)*
global_stmt:            'global' NAME (',' NAME)*
nonlocal_stmt:          'nonlocal' NAME (',' NAME)*
assert_stmt:            'assert' test [',' test]

compound_stmt:          if_stmt | while_stmt | for_stmt |
                        try_stmt | with_stmt | funcdef |
                        classdef | decorated
if_stmt:                'if' test ':' suite ('elif' test ':'
                        suite)* ['else' ':' suite]
while_stmt:             'while' test ':' suite ['else' ':'
                        suite]
for_stmt:               'for' exprlist 'in' testlist ':'
                        suite ['else' ':' suite]
try_stmt:               ('try' ':' suite ((except_clause ':'
                        suite)+ ['else' ':' suite] ['finally'
                        ':' suite] | 'finally' ':' suite))
with_stmt:              'with' with_item (',' with_item)* ':'
                        suite
with_item:              test ['as' expr]

# NB compile.c makes sure that the default except clause is
# last

except_clause:          'except' [test ['as' NAME]]
suite:                  simple_stmt | NEWLINE INDENT stmt+
                        DEDENT

test:                   or_test ['if' or_test 'else' test] |
                        lambdef
test_nocond:            or_test | lambdef_nocond
lambdef:                'lambda' [varargslist] ':' test
lambdef_nocond:         'lambda' [varargslist] ':'
                        test_nocond
```

```
or_test:              and_test ('or' and_test)*
and_test:             not_test ('and' not_test)*
not_test:             'not' not_test | comparison
comparison:           expr (comp_op expr)*
comp_op:              '<'|'>'|'=='|'>='|'<='|'<>'|'!='|'in'|'not'
                      'in'|'is'|'is' 'not'
star_expr:            '*' expr
expr:                 xor_expr ('|' xor_expr)*
xor_expr:             and_expr ('^' and_expr)*
and_expr:             shift_expr ('&' shift_expr)*
shift_expr:           arith_expr (('<<'|'>>') arith_expr)*
arith_expr:           term (('+'|'-') term)*
term:                 factor (('*'|'/'|'%'|'//') factor)*
factor:               ('+'|'-'|'~') factor | power
power:                atom trailer* ['**' factor]
atom:                 ('(' [yield_expr|testlist_comp]
                      ')' | '[' [testlist_comp] ']' | '{'
                      [dictorsetmaker] '}' | NAME | NUMBER |
                      STRING+ | '...' | 'None' | 'True' |
                      'False')
testlist_comp:        (test|star_expr) ( comp_for | (','
                      (test|star_expr))* [','] )
trailer:              '(' [arglist] ')' | '[' subscriptlist
                      ']' | '.' NAME
subscriptlist:        subscript (',' subscript)* [',']
subscript:            test | [test] ':' [test] [sliceop]
sliceop:              ':' [test]
exprlist:             (expr|star_expr) (','
                      (expr|star_expr))* [',']
testlist:             test (',' test)* [',']
dictorsetmaker:       ( (test ':' test (comp_for | (','
                      test ':' test)* [','])) | (test
                      (comp_for | (',' test)* [','])) )

classdef:             'class' NAME ['(' [arglist] ')'] ':'
                      suite

arglist:              (argument ',')* (argument [','] |'*'
                      test (',' argument)* [',' '**' test]
                      |'**' test)

# The reason that keywords are test nodes instead of NAME
# is that using NAME results in an ambiguity.  ast.c makes
# sure it's a NAME.

argument:             test [comp_for] | test '=' test
                          # Really [keyword '='] test
```

```
comp_iter:          comp_for | comp_if
comp_for:           'for' exprlist 'in' or_test
                    [comp_iter]
comp_if:            'if' test_nocond [comp_iter]

# not used in grammar, but may appear in "node" passed from
# Parser to Compiler

encoding_decl:      NAME

yield_expr:         'yield' [testlist]
```

A. About these documents

These documents are generated from reStructuredText[1] sources by Sphinx[2], a document processor specifically written for the Python documentation.

Development of the documentation and its toolchain takes place on the docs@python.org mailing list. We're always looking for volunteers wanting to help with the docs, so feel free to send a mail there!

Many thanks go to:

- Fred L. Drake, Jr., the creator of the original Python documentation toolset and writer of much of the content;
- the Docutils[3] project for creating reStructuredText and the Docutils suite;
- Fredrik Lundh for his Alternative Python Reference[4] project from which Sphinx got many good ideas.

A.1. Contributors to the Python Documentation

This section lists people who have contributed in some way to the Python documentation. It is probably not complete – if you feel that you or anyone else should be on this list, please let us know (send email to docs@python.org), and we'll be glad to correct the problem.

Aahz, Michael Abbott, Steve Alexander, Jim Ahlstrom, Fred Allen, A. Amoroso, Pehr Anderson, Oliver Andrich, Heidi Annexstad, Jesús Cea Avión, Manuel Balsera, Daniel Barclay, Chris Barker, Don Bashford, Anthony Baxter, Alexander Belopolsky, Bennett Benson, Jonathan Black, Robin Boerdijk, Michal Bozon, Aaron Brancotti, Georg Brandl, Keith Briggs, Ian Bruntlett, Lee Busby, Lorenzo M. Catucci, Carl Cerecke, Mauro Cicognini, Gilles Civario, Mike Clarkson, Steve Clift, Dave Cole, Matthew Cowles, Jeremy Craven, Andrew Dalke, Ben Darnell, L. Peter Deutsch, Robert Donohue, Fred L. Drake, Jr., Jacques Ducasse, Josip Dzolonga, Jeff Epler, Michael Ernst, Blame Andy Eskilsson, Carey Evans, Martijn Faassen, Carl Feynman, Dan Finnie, Hernán Martínez Foffani, Stefan Franke, Jim Fulton, Peter Funk, Lele Gaifax, Matthew Gallagher, Gabriel Genellina, Ben Gertzfield, Nadim Ghaznavi, Jonathan Giddy, Matt Giuca, Shelley Gooch, Nathaniel Gray, Grant Griffin, Thomas Guettler, Anders Hammarquist, Mark Hammond, Harald Hanche-Olsen, Manus Hand, Gerhard Häring, Travis B. Hartwell, Tim Hatch, Janko Hauser, Thomas Heller, Bernhard Herzog, Magnus L. Hetland, Konrad Hinsen, Stefan Hoffmeister, Albert Hofkamp, Gregor Hoffleit, Steve Holden, Thomas Holenstein, Gerrit

---

[1] http://docutils.sf.net/rst.html
[2] http://sphinx.pocoo.org/
[3] http://docutils.sf.net/
[4] http://effbot.org/zone/pyref.htm

Holl, Rob Hooft, Brian Hooper, Randall Hopper, Michael Hudson, Eric Huss, Jeremy Hylton, Roger Irwin, Jack Jansen, Philip H. Jensen, Pedro Diaz Jimenez, Kent Johnson, Lucas de Jonge, Andreas Jung, Robert Kern, Jim Kerr, Jan Kim, Greg Kochanski, Guido Kollerie, Peter A. Koren, Daniel Kozan, Andrew M. Kuchling, Dave Kuhlman, Erno Kuusela, Ross Lagerwall, Thomas Lamb, Detlef Lannert, Piers Lauder, Glyph Lefkowitz, Robert Lehmann, Marc-André Lemburg, Ross Light, Ulf A. Lindgren, Everett Lipman, Mirko Liss, Martin von Löwis, Fredrik Lundh, Jeff MacDonald, John Machin, Andrew MacIntyre, Vladimir Marangozov, Vincent Marchetti, Westley Martínez, Laura Matson, Daniel May, Rebecca McCreary, Doug Mennella, Paolo Milani, Skip Montanaro, Paul Moore, Ross Moore, Sjoerd Mullender, Dale Nagata, Michal Nowikowski, Ng Pheng Siong, Koray Oner, Tomas Oppelstrup, Denis S. Otkidach, Zooko O'Whielacronx, Shriphani Palakodety, William Park, Joonas Paalasmaa, Harri Pasanen, Bo Peng, Tim Peters, Benjamin Peterson, Christopher Petrilli, Justin D. Pettit, Chris Phoenix, François Pinard, Paul Prescod, Eric S. Raymond, Edward K. Ream, Terry J. Reedy, Sean Reifschneider, Bernhard Reiter, Armin Rigo, Wes Rishel, Armin Ronacher, Jim Roskind, Guido van Rossum, Donald Wallace Rouse II, Mark Russell, Nick Russo, Chris Ryland, Constantina S., Hugh Sasse, Bob Savage, Scott Schram, Neil Schemenauer, Barry Scott, Joakim Sernbrant, Justin Sheehy, Charlie Shepherd, SilentGhost, Michael Simcich, Ionel Simionescu, Michael Sloan, Gregory P. Smith, Roy Smith, Clay Spence, Nicholas Spies, Tage Stabell-Kulo, Frank Stajano, Anthony Starks, Greg Stein, Peter Stoehr, Mark Summerfield, Reuben Sumner, Kalle Svensson, Jim Tittsler, David Turner, Ville Vainio, Martijn Vries, Charles G. Waldman, Greg Ward, Barry Warsaw, Corran Webster, Glyn Webster, Bob Weiner, Eddy Welbourne, Jeff Wheeler, Mats Wichmann, Gerry Wiener, Timothy Wild, Paul Winkler, Collin Winter, Blake Winton, Dan Wolfe, Steven Work, Thomas Wouters, Ka-Ping Yee, Rory Yorke, Moshe Zadka, Milan Zamazal, Cheng Zhang, Trent Nelson, Michael Foord.

It is only with the input and contributions of the Python community that Python has such wonderful documentation – Thank You!

B. History and License

B.1. History of the software

Python was created in the early 1990s by Guido van Rossum at Stichting Mathematisch Centrum (CWI, see http://www.cwi.nl/) in the Netherlands as a successor of a language called ABC. Guido remains Python's principal author, although it includes many contributions from others.

In 1995, Guido continued his work on Python at the Corporation for National Research Initiatives (CNRI, see http://www.cnri.reston.va.us/) in Reston, Virginia where he released several versions of the software.

In May 2000, Guido and the Python core development team moved to BeOpen.com to form the BeOpen PythonLabs team. In October of the same year, the PythonLabs team moved to Digital Creations (now Zope Corporation; see http://www.zope.com/). In 2001, the Python Software Foundation (PSF, see http://www.python.org/psf/) was formed, a non-profit organization created specifically to own Python-related Intellectual Property. Zope Corporation is a sponsoring member of the PSF.

All Python releases are Open Source (see http://www.opensource.org/ for the Open Source Definition). Historically, most, but not all, Python releases have also been GPL-compatible; the table below summarizes the various releases.

Release	Derived from	Year	Owner	GPL compatible?
0.9.0 thru 1.2	n/a	1991-1995	CWI	yes
1.3 thru 1.5.2	1.2	1995-1999	CNRI	yes
1.6	1.5.2	2000	CNRI	no
2.0	1.6	2000	BeOpen.com	no
1.6.1	1.6	2001	CNRI	no
2.1	2.0+1.6.1	2001	PSF	no
2.0.1	2.0+1.6.1	2001	PSF	yes
2.1.1	2.1+2.0.1	2001	PSF	yes
2.2	2.1.1	2001	PSF	yes
2.1.2	2.1.1	2002	PSF	yes
2.1.3	2.1.2	2002	PSF	yes
2.2.1	2.2	2002	PSF	yes
2.2.2	2.2.1	2002	PSF	yes
2.2.3	2.2.2	2002-2003	PSF	yes
2.3	2.2.2	2002-2003	PSF	yes
2.3.1	2.3	2002-2003	PSF	yes
2.3.2	2.3.1	2003	PSF	yes
				Continued on next page

Continued on next page

Table B.1 – continued from previous page

2.3.3	2.3.2	2003	PSF	yes
2.3.4	2.3.3	2004	PSF	yes
2.3.5	2.3.4	2005	PSF	yes
2.4	2.3	2004	PSF	yes
2.4.1	2.4	2005	PSF	yes
2.4.2	2.4.1	2005	PSF	yes
2.4.3	2.4.2	2006	PSF	yes
2.4.4	2.4.3	2006	PSF	yes
2.5	2.4	2006	PSF	yes
2.5.1	2.5	2007	PSF	yes
2.6	2.5	2008	PSF	yes
2.6.1	2.6	2008	PSF	yes
2.6.2	2.6.1	2009	PSF	yes
2.6.3	2.6.2	2009	PSF	yes
2.6.4	2.6.3	2009	PSF	yes
3.0	2.6	2008	PSF	yes
3.0.1	3.0	2009	PSF	yes
3.1	3.0.1	2009	PSF	yes
3.1.1	3.1	2009	PSF	yes
3.1.2	3.1	2010	PSF	yes
3.2	3.1	2011	PSF	yes

Note: GPL-compatible doesn't mean that we're distributing Python under the GPL. All Python licenses, unlike the GPL, let you distribute a modified version without making your changes open source. The GPL-compatible licenses make it possible to combine Python with other software that is released under the GPL; the others don't.

Thanks to the many outside volunteers who have worked under Guido's direction to make these releases possible.

B.2. Terms and conditions for accessing or otherwise using Python

PSF LICENSE AGREEMENT FOR PYTHON 3.2

1. This LICENSE AGREEMENT is between the Python Software Foundation ("PSF"), and the Individual or Organization ("Licensee") accessing and otherwise using Python 3.2 software in source or binary form and its associated documentation.

2. Subject to the terms and conditions of this License Agreement, PSF hereby grants Licensee a nonexclusive, royalty-free, world-wide license to reproduce, analyze, test, perform and/or display publicly, prepare derivative works, distribute, and otherwise use Python 3.2 alone or in any derivative version, provided, however, that PSF's License Agreement and PSF's notice of copyright, i.e., "Copyright © 2001-2011 Python Software Foundation; All Rights Reserved" are retained in Python 3.2 alone or in any derivative version prepared by Licensee.

3. In the event Licensee prepares a derivative work that is based on or incorporates Python 3.2 or any part thereof, and wants to make the derivative work available to

others as provided herein, then Licensee hereby agrees to include in any such work a brief summary of the changes made to Python 3.2.

4. PSF is making Python 3.2 available to Licensee on an "AS IS" basis. PSF MAKES NO REPRESENTATIONS OR WARRANTIES, EXPRESS OR IMPLIED. BY WAY OF EXAMPLE, BUT NOT LIMITATION, PSF MAKES NO AND DISCLAIMS ANY REPRESENTATION OR WARRANTY OF MERCHANTABILITY OR FITNESS FOR ANY PARTICULAR PURPOSE OR THAT THE USE OF PYTHON 3.2 WILL NOT INFRINGE ANY THIRD PARTY RIGHTS.

5. PSF SHALL NOT BE LIABLE TO LICENSEE OR ANY OTHER USERS OF PYTHON 3.2 FOR ANY INCIDENTAL, SPECIAL, OR CONSEQUENTIAL DAMAGES OR LOSS AS A RESULT OF MODIFYING, DISTRIBUTING, OR OTHERWISE USING PYTHON 3.2, OR ANY DERIVATIVE THEREOF, EVEN IF ADVISED OF THE POSSIBILITY THEREOF.

6. This License Agreement will automatically terminate upon a material breach of its terms and conditions.

7. Nothing in this License Agreement shall be deemed to create any relationship of agency, partnership, or joint venture between PSF and Licensee. This License Agreement does not grant permission to use PSF trademarks or trade name in a trademark sense to endorse or promote products or services of Licensee, or any third party.

8. By copying, installing or otherwise using Python 3.2, Licensee agrees to be bound by the terms and conditions of this License Agreement.

BEOPEN.COM LICENSE AGREEMENT FOR PYTHON 2.0

BEOPEN PYTHON OPEN SOURCE LICENSE AGREEMENT VERSION 1

1. This LICENSE AGREEMENT is between BeOpen.com ("BeOpen"), having an office at 160 Saratoga Avenue, Santa Clara, CA 95051, and the Individual or Organization ("Licensee") accessing and otherwise using this software in source or binary form and its associated documentation ("the Software").

2. Subject to the terms and conditions of this BeOpen Python License Agreement, BeOpen hereby grants Licensee a non-exclusive, royalty-free, world-wide license to reproduce, analyze, test, perform and/or display publicly, prepare derivative works, distribute, and otherwise use the Software alone or in any derivative version, provided, however, that the BeOpen Python License is retained in the Software, alone or in any derivative version prepared by Licensee.

3. BeOpen is making the Software available to Licensee on an "AS IS" basis. BEOPEN MAKES NO REPRESENTATIONS OR WARRANTIES, EXPRESS OR IMPLIED. BY WAY OF EXAMPLE, BUT NOT LIMITATION, BEOPEN MAKES NO AND DISCLAIMS ANY REPRESENTATION OR WARRANTY OF MERCHANTABILITY OR FITNESS FOR ANY PARTICULAR PURPOSE OR THAT THE USE OF THE SOFTWARE WILL NOT INFRINGE ANY THIRD PARTY RIGHTS.

4. BEOPEN SHALL NOT BE LIABLE TO LICENSEE OR ANY OTHER USERS OF THE SOFTWARE FOR ANY INCIDENTAL, SPECIAL, OR CONSEQUENTIAL DAMAGES OR LOSS AS A RESULT OF USING, MODIFYING OR DISTRIBUTING THE SOFTWARE, OR ANY DERIVATIVE THEREOF, EVEN IF ADVISED OF THE POSSIBILITY THEREOF.

5. This License Agreement will automatically terminate upon a material breach of its terms and conditions.

6. This License Agreement shall be governed by and interpreted in all respects by the law of the State of California, excluding conflict of law provisions. Nothing in this License Agreement shall be deemed to create any relationship of agency, partnership, or joint venture between BeOpen and Licensee. This License Agreement does not grant permission to use BeOpen trademarks or trade names in a trademark sense to endorse or promote products or services of Licensee, or any third party. As an exception, the "BeOpen Python" logos available at http://www.pythonlabs.com/logos.html may be used according to the permissions granted on that web page.

7. By copying, installing or otherwise using the software, Licensee agrees to be bound by the terms and conditions of this License Agreement.

CNRI LICENSE AGREEMENT FOR PYTHON 1.6.1

1. This LICENSE AGREEMENT is between the Corporation for National Research Initiatives, having an office at 1895 Preston White Drive, Reston, VA 20191 ("CNRI"), and the Individual or Organization ("Licensee") accessing and otherwise using Python 1.6.1 software in source or binary form and its associated documentation.

2. Subject to the terms and conditions of this License Agreement, CNRI hereby grants Licensee a nonexclusive, royalty-free, world-wide license to reproduce, analyze, test, perform and/or display publicly, prepare derivative works, distribute, and otherwise use Python 1.6.1 alone or in any derivative version, provided, however, that CNRI's License Agreement and CNRI's notice of copyright, i.e., "Copyright © 1995-2001 Corporation for National Research Initiatives; All Rights Reserved" are retained in Python 1.6.1 alone or in any derivative version prepared by Licensee. Alternately, in lieu of CNRI's License Agreement, Licensee may substitute the following text (omitting the quotes): "Python 1.6.1 is made available subject to the terms and conditions in CNRI's License Agreement. This Agreement together with Python 1.6.1 may be located on the Internet using the following unique, persistent identifier (known as a handle): 1895.22/1013. This Agreement may also be obtained from a proxy server on the Internet using the following URL: http://hdl.handle.net/1895.22/1013."

3. In the event Licensee prepares a derivative work that is based on or incorporates Python 1.6.1 or any part thereof, and wants to make the derivative work available to others as provided herein, then Licensee hereby agrees to include in any such work a brief summary of the changes made to Python 1.6.1.

4. CNRI is making Python 1.6.1 available to Licensee on an "AS IS" basis. CNRI MAKES NO REPRESENTATIONS OR WARRANTIES, EXPRESS OR IMPLIED. BY WAY OF EXAMPLE, BUT NOT LIMITATION, CNRI MAKES NO AND DISCLAIMS ANY REPRESENTATION OR WARRANTY OF MERCHANTABILITY OR FITNESS FOR ANY PARTICULAR PURPOSE OR THAT THE USE OF PYTHON 1.6.1 WILL NOT INFRINGE ANY THIRD PARTY RIGHTS.

5. CNRI SHALL NOT BE LIABLE TO LICENSEE OR ANY OTHER USERS OF PYTHON 1.6.1 FOR ANY INCIDENTAL, SPECIAL, OR CONSEQUENTIAL DAMAGES OR LOSS AS A RESULT OF MODIFYING, DISTRIBUTING, OR OTHERWISE USING PYTHON 1.6.1, OR ANY DERIVATIVE THEREOF, EVEN IF ADVISED OF THE POSSIBILITY THEREOF.

6. This License Agreement will automatically terminate upon a material breach of its terms and conditions.

7. This License Agreement shall be governed by the federal intellectual property law of the United States, including without limitation the federal copyright law, and, to the extent such U.S. federal law does not apply, by the law of the Commonwealth of Virginia, excluding Virginia's conflict of law provisions. Notwithstanding the foregoing, with regard to derivative works based on Python 1.6.1 that incorporate nonseparable material that was previously distributed under the GNU General Public License (GPL), the law of the Commonwealth of Virginia shall govern this License Agreement only as to issues arising under or with respect to Paragraphs 4, 5, and 7 of this License Agreement. Nothing in this License Agreement shall be deemed to create any relationship of agency, partnership, or joint venture between CNRI and Licensee. This License Agreement does not grant permission to use CNRI trademarks or trade name in a trademark sense to endorse or promote products or services of Licensee, or any third party.

8. By clicking on the "ACCEPT" button where indicated, or by copying, installing or otherwise using Python 1.6.1, Licensee agrees to be bound by the terms and conditions of this License Agreement.

ACCEPT

CWI LICENSE AGREEMENT FOR PYTHON 0.9.0 THROUGH 1.2

B.3. Licenses and Acknowledgements for Incorporated Software

This section is an incomplete, but growing list of licenses and acknowledgements for third-party software incorporated in the Python distribution.

B.3.1. Mersenne Twister

The _random module includes code based on a download from http://www.math.keio.ac.jp/matumoto/MT2002/emt19937ar.html. The following are the verbatim comments from the original code:

A C-program for MT19937, with initialization improved 2002/1/26. Coded by Takuji Nishimura and Makoto Matsumoto.

Before using, initialize the state by using init_genrand(seed) or init_by_array(init_key, key_length).

OF USE, DATA, OR PROFITS; OR BUSINESS INTERRUPTION) HOWEVER CAUSED AND ON ANY THEORY OF LIABILITY, WHETHER IN CONTRACT, STRICT LIABILITY, OR TORT (INCLUDING NEGLIGENCE OR OTHERWISE) ARISING IN ANY WAY OUT OF THE USE OF THIS SOFTWARE, EVEN IF ADVISED OF THE POSSIBILITY OF SUCH DAMAGE.

Any feedback is very welcome. http://www.math.keio.ac.jp/matumoto/emt.html email: matumoto@math.keio.ac.jp

B.3.2. Sockets

The socket module uses the functions, getaddrinfo(), and getnameinfo(), which are coded in separate source files from the WIDE Project, http://www.wide.ad.jp/.

Copyright (C) 1995, 1996, 1997, and 1998 WIDE Project. All rights reserved.

Redistribution and use in source and binary forms, with or without modification, are permitted provided that the following conditions are met:

1. Redistributions of source code must retain the above copyright notice, this list of conditions and the following disclaimer.

2. Redistributions in binary form must reproduce the above copyright notice, this list of conditions and the following disclaimer in the documentation and/or other materials provided with the distribution.

3. Neither the name of the project nor the names of its contributors may be used to endorse or promote products derived from this software without specific prior written permission.

THIS SOFTWARE IS PROVIDED BY THE PROJECT AND CONTRIBUTORS "AS IS" AND GAI ANY EXPRESS OR IMPLIED WARRANTIES, INCLUDING, BUT NOT LIMITED TO, THE IMPLIED WARRANTIES OF MERCHANTABILITY AND FITNESS FOR A PARTICULAR PURPOSE ARE DISCLAIMED. IN NO EVENT SHALL THE PROJECT OR CONTRIBUTORS BE LIABLE FOR GAI ANY DIRECT, INDIRECT, INCIDENTAL, SPECIAL, EXEMPLARY, OR CONSEQUENTIAL DAMAGES (INCLUDING, BUT NOT LIMITED TO, PROCUREMENT OF SUBSTITUTE GOODS OR SERVICES; LOSS OF USE, DATA, OR PROFITS; OR BUSINESS INTERRUPTION) HOWEVER CAUSED AND ON GAI ANY THEORY OF LIABILITY, WHETHER IN CONTRACT, STRICT LIABILITY, OR TORT (INCLUDING NEGLIGENCE OR OTHERWISE) ARISING IN GAI ANY WAY OUT OF THE USE OF THIS SOFTWARE, EVEN IF ADVISED OF THE POSSIBILITY OF SUCH DAMAGE.

B.3.3. Floating point exception control

The source for the fpectl module includes the following notice:

Copyright (c) 1996. The Regents of the University of California. All rights reserved.

Permission to use, copy, modify, and distribute this software for any purpose without fee is hereby granted, provided that this en- tire notice is included in all copies of any software which is or includes a copy or modification of this software and in all copies of the supporting documentation for such software.

This work was produced at the University of California, Lawrence Livermore National Laboratory under contract no. W-7405-ENG-48 between the U.S. Department of Energy and The Regents of the University of California for the operation of UC LLNL.

DISCLAIMER

This software was prepared as an account of work sponsored by an agency of the United States Government. Neither the United States Government nor the University of California nor any of their em- ployees, makes any warranty, express or implied, or assumes any liability or responsibility for the accuracy, completeness, or usefulness of any information, apparatus, product, or process disclosed, or represents that its use would not infringe privately-owned rights. Reference herein to any specific commer- cial products, process, or service by trade name, trademark, manufacturer, or otherwise, does not necessarily constitute or imply its endorsement, recommendation, or favoring by the United States Government or the University of California. The views and opinions of authors expressed herein do not necessarily state or reflect those of the United States Government or the University of California, and shall not be used for advertising or product endorsement purposes.

B.3.4. Asynchronous socket services

The asynchat and asyncore modules contain the following notice:

Copyright 1996 by Sam Rushing

All Rights Reserved

Permission to use, copy, modify, and distribute this software and its documentation for any purpose and without fee is hereby granted, provided that the above copyright notice appear in all copies and that both that copyright notice and this permission notice appear in supporting documentation, and that the name of Sam Rushing not be used in advertising or publicity pertaining to distribution of the software without specific, written prior permission.

SAM RUSHING DISCLAIMS ALL WARRANTIES WITH REGARD TO THIS SOFTWARE, INCLUDING ALL IMPLIED WARRANTIES OF MERCHANTABIL- ITY AND FITNESS, IN NO EVENT SHALL SAM RUSHING BE LIABLE FOR ANY SPECIAL, INDIRECT OR CONSEQUENTIAL DAMAGES OR ANY DAM- AGES WHATSOEVER RESULTING FROM LOSS OF USE, DATA OR PROFITS, WHETHER IN AN ACTION OF CONTRACT, NEGLIGENCE OR OTHER TOR- TIOUS ACTION, ARISING OUT OF OR IN CONNECTION WITH THE USE OR PERFORMANCE OF THIS SOFTWARE.

B.3.5. Cookie management

The http.cookies module contains the following notice:

Copyright 2000 by Timothy O'Malley <timo@alum.mit.edu>

All Rights Reserved

Permission to use, copy, modify, and distribute this software and its documentation for any purpose and without fee is hereby granted, provided that the above copyright notice appear in all copies and that both that copyright notice and this permission notice appear in supporting documentation, and that the name of Timothy O'Malley not be used in advertising or publicity pertaining to distribution of the software without specific, written prior permission.

Timothy O'Malley DISCLAIMS ALL WARRANTIES WITH REGARD TO THIS SOFTWARE, INCLUDING ALL IMPLIED WARRANTIES OF MERCHANTABIL- ITY AND FITNESS, IN NO EVENT SHALL Timothy O'Malley BE LIABLE FOR ANY SPECIAL, INDIRECT OR CONSEQUENTIAL DAMAGES OR ANY DAM- AGES WHATSOEVER RESULTING FROM LOSS OF USE, DATA OR PROFITS, WHETHER IN AN ACTION OF CONTRACT, NEGLIGENCE OR OTHER TOR- TIOUS ACTION, ARISING OUT OF OR IN CONNECTION WITH THE USE OR PERFORMANCE OF THIS SOFTWARE.

B.3.6. Profiling

The profile and pstats modules contain the following notice:

Copyright 1994, by InfoSeek Corporation, all rights reserved. Written by James Roskind

Permission to use, copy, modify, and distribute this Python software and its associated documentation for any purpose (subject to the restriction in the following sentence) without fee is hereby granted, provided that the above copyright notice appears in all copies, and that both that copyright notice and this permission notice appear in supporting documentation, and that the name of InfoSeek not be used in advertising or publicity pertaining to distribution of the software without specific, written prior permission. This permission is explicitly restricted to the copying and modification of the software to remain in Python, compiled Python, or other languages (such as C) wherein the modified or derived code is exclusively imported into a Python module.

INFOSEEK CORPORATION DISCLAIMS ALL WARRANTIES WITH REGARD TO THIS SOFTWARE, INCLUDING ALL IMPLIED WARRANTIES OF MERCHANTABILITY AND FITNESS. IN NO EVENT SHALL INFOSEEK CORPORATION BE LIABLE FOR ANY SPECIAL, INDIRECT OR CONSEQUENTIAL DAMAGES OR ANY DAMAGES WHATSOEVER RESULTING FROM LOSS OF USE, DATA OR PROFITS, WHETHER IN AN ACTION OF CONTRACT, NEGLIGENCE OR OTHER TORTIOUS ACTION, ARISING OUT OF OR IN CONNECTION WITH THE USE OR PERFORMANCE OF THIS SOFTWARE.

B.3.7. Execution tracing

The trace module contains the following notice:

portions copyright 2001, Autonomous Zones Industries, Inc., all rights... err... reserved and offered to the public under the terms of the Python 2.2 license. Author: Zooko O'Whielacronx http://zooko.com/ mailto:zooko@zooko.com

Copyright 2000, Mojam Media, Inc., all rights reserved. Author: Skip Montanaro

Copyright 1999, Bioreason, Inc., all rights reserved. Author: Andrew Dalke

Copyright 1995-1997, Automatrix, Inc., all rights reserved. Author: Skip Montanaro

Copyright 1991-1995, Stichting Mathematisch Centrum, all rights reserved.

Permission to use, copy, modify, and distribute this Python software and its associated documentation for any purpose without fee is hereby granted, provided that the above copyright notice appears in all copies, and that both that copyright notice and this permission notice appear in supporting documentation, and that the name of neither Automatrix, Bioreason or Mojam Media be used in advertising or publicity pertaining to distribution of the software without specific, written prior permission.

B.3.8. UUencode and UUdecode functions

The uu module contains the following notice:

Copyright 1994 by Lance Ellinghouse

Cathedral City, California Republic, United States of America. All Rights Reserved

Permission to use, copy, modify, and distribute this software and its documentation for any purpose and without fee is hereby granted, provided that the above copyright notice appear in all copies and that both that copyright notice and this permission notice appear in supporting documentation, and that the name of Lance Ellinghouse not be used in advertising or publicity pertaining to distribution of the software without specific, written prior permission.

LANCE ELLINGHOUSE DISCLAIMS ALL WARRANTIES WITH REGARD TO THIS SOFTWARE, INCLUDING ALL IMPLIED WARRANTIES OF MERCHANTABILITY AND FITNESS, IN NO EVENT SHALL LANCE ELLINGHOUSE CENTRUM BE LIABLE FOR ANY SPECIAL, INDIRECT OR CONSEQUENTIAL DAMAGES OR ANY DAMAGES WHATSOEVER RESULTING FROM LOSS OF USE, DATA OR PROFITS, WHETHER IN AN ACTION OF CONTRACT, NEGLIGENCE OR OTHER TORTIOUS ACTION, ARISING OUT OF OR IN CONNECTION WITH THE USE OR PERFORMANCE OF THIS SOFTWARE.

Modified by Jack Jansen, CWI, July 1995: - Use binascii module to do the actual line-by-line conversion between ascii and binary. This results in a 1000-fold speedup. The C version is still 5 times faster, though. - Arguments more compliant with Python standard

B.3.9. XML Remote Procedure Calls

The xmlrpc.client module contains the following notice:

The XML-RPC client interface is

Copyright (c) 1999-2002 by Secret Labs AB Copyright (c) 1999-2002 by Fredrik Lundh

By obtaining, using, and/or copying this software and/or its associated documentation, you agree that you have read, understood, and will comply with the following terms and conditions:

Permission to use, copy, modify, and distribute this software and its associated documentation for any purpose and without fee is hereby granted, provided that the above copyright notice appears in all copies, and that both that copyright notice and this permission notice appear in supporting documentation, and that the name of Secret Labs AB or the author not be used in advertising or publicity pertaining to distribution of the software without specific, written prior permission.

SECRET LABS AB AND THE AUTHOR DISCLAIMS ALL WARRANTIES WITH REGARD TO THIS SOFTWARE, INCLUDING ALL IMPLIED WARRANTIES OF MERCHANT- ABILITY AND FITNESS. IN NO EVENT SHALL SECRET LABS AB OR THE AUTHOR BE LIABLE FOR ANY SPECIAL, INDIRECT OR CONSEQUENTIAL DAMAGES OR ANY DAMAGES WHATSOEVER RESULTING FROM LOSS OF USE, DATA OR PROFITS, WHETHER IN AN ACTION OF CONTRACT, NEGLIGENCE OR OTHER TORTIOUS ACTION, ARISING OUT OF OR IN CONNECTION WITH THE USE OR PERFORMANCE OF THIS SOFTWARE.

B.3.10. test_epoll

The test_epoll contains the following notice:

Copyright (c) 2001-2006 Twisted Matrix Laboratories.

Permission is hereby granted, free of charge, to any person obtaining a copy of this software and associated documentation files (the "Software"), to deal in the Software without restriction, including without limitation the rights to use, copy, modify, merge, publish, distribute, sublicense, and/or sell copies of the Software, and to permit persons to whom the Software is furnished to do so, subject to the following conditions:

The above copyright notice and this permission notice shall be included in all copies or substantial portions of the Software.

THE SOFTWARE IS PROVIDED "AS IS", WITHOUT WARRANTY OF ANY KIND, EXPRESS OR IMPLIED, INCLUDING BUT NOT LIMITED TO THE WARRANTIES OF MERCHANTABILITY, FITNESS FOR A PARTICULAR PURPOSE

B.3.11. Select kqueue

The select and contains the following notice for the kqueue interface:

B.3.12. strtod and dtoa

The file Python/dtoa.c, which supplies C functions dtoa and strtod for conversion of C doubles to and from strings, is derived from the file of the same name by David M. Gay, currently available from http://www.netlib.org/fp/. The original file, as retrieved on March 16, 2009, contains the following copyright and licensing notice:

The author of this software is David M. Gay.

B.3.13. OpenSSL

The modules `hashlib`, `posix`, `ssl`, `crypt` use the OpenSSL library for added performance if made available by the operating system. Additionally, the Windows installers for Python include a copy of the OpenSSL libraries, so we include a copy of the OpenSSL license here:

LICENSE ISSUES

The OpenSSL toolkit stays under a dual license, i.e. both the conditions of the OpenSSL License and the original SSLeay license apply to the toolkit. See below for the actual license texts. Actually both licenses are BSD-style Open Source licenses. In case of any license issues related to OpenSSL please contact openssl-core@openssl.org.

OpenSSL License

Copyright (c) 1998-2008 The OpenSSL Project. All rights reserved.

Redistribution and use in source and binary forms, with or without modification, are permitted provided that the following conditions are met:

1. Redistributions of source code must retain the above copyright notice, this list of conditions and the following disclaimer.

2. Redistributions in binary form must reproduce the above copyright notice, this list of conditions and the following disclaimer in the documentation and/or other materials provided with the distribution.

3. All advertising materials mentioning features or use of this software must display the following acknowledgment: "This product includes software developed by the OpenSSL Project for use in the OpenSSL Toolkit.[1]"

4. The names "OpenSSL Toolkit" and "OpenSSL Project" must not be used to endorse or promote products derived from this software without prior written permission. For written permission, please contact openssl-core@openssl.org.

5. Products derived from this software may not be called "OpenSSL" nor may "OpenSSL" appear in their names without prior written permission of the OpenSSL Project.

6. Redistributions of any form whatsoever must retain the following acknowledgment: "This product includes software developed by the OpenSSL Project for use in the OpenSSL Toolkit"

THIS SOFTWARE IS PROVIDED BY THE OpenSSL PROJECT "AS IS" AND ANY EXPRESSED OR IMPLIED WARRANTIES, INCLUDING, BUT NOT LIMITED TO, THE IMPLIED WARRANTIES OF MERCHANTABILITY AND FITNESS FOR A PARTICULAR PURPOSE ARE DISCLAIMED. IN NO EVENT SHALL THE OpenSSL PROJECT OR ITS CONTRIBUTORS BE LIABLE FOR ANY DIRECT, INDIRECT, INCIDENTAL, SPECIAL, EXEMPLARY, OR CONSEQUENTIAL DAMAGES (INCLUDING, BUT NOT LIMITED TO, PROCUREMENT OF SUBSTITUTE GOODS OR SERVICES; LOSS OF USE, DATA, OR PROFITS; OR BUSINESS INTERRUPTION) HOWEVER CAUSED AND ON ANY THEORY OF LIABILITY, WHETHER IN CONTRACT, STRICT LIABILITY, OR TORT (INCLUDING NEGLIGENCE OR OTHERWISE) ARISING IN ANY WAY OUT OF THE USE OF THIS SOFTWARE, EVEN IF ADVISED OF THE POSSIBILITY OF SUCH DAMAGE.

This product includes cryptographic software written by Eric Young (eay@cryptsoft.com). This product includes software written by Tim Hudson (tjh@cryptsoft.com).

---

[1] http://www.openssl.org/

Original SSLeay License

Copyright (C) 1995-1998 Eric Young (eay@cryptsoft.com) All rights reserved.

This package is an SSL implementation written by Eric Young (eay@cryptsoft.com). The implementation was written so as to conform with Netscapes SSL.

This library is free for commercial and non-commercial use as long as the following conditions are aheared to. The following conditions apply to all code found in this distribution, be it the RC4, RSA, lhash, DES, etc., code; not just the SSL code. The SSL documentation included with this distribution is covered by the same copyright terms except that the holder is Tim Hudson (tjh@cryptsoft.com).

Copyright remains Eric Young's, and as such any Copyright notices in the code are not to be removed. If this package is used in a product, Eric Young should be given attribution as the author of the parts of the library used. This can be in the form of a textual message at program startup or in documentation (online or textual) provided with the package.

Redistribution and use in source and binary forms, with or without modification, are permitted provided that the following conditions are met:

1. Redistributions of source code must retain the copyright notice, this list of conditions and the following disclaimer.

2. Redistributions in binary form must reproduce the above copyright notice, this list of conditions and the following disclaimer in the documentation and/or other materials provided with the distribution.

3. All advertising materials mentioning features or use of this software must display the following acknowledgement: "This product includes cryptographic software written by Eric Young (eay@cryptsoft.com)" The word 'cryptographic' can be left out if the rouines from the library being used are not cryptographic related :-).

4. If you include any Windows specific code (or a derivative thereof) from the apps directory (application code) you must include an acknowledgement: "This product includes software written by Tim Hudson (tjh@cryptsoft.com)"

THIS SOFTWARE IS PROVIDED BY ERIC YOUNG "AS IS" AND ANY EXPRESS OR IMPLIED WARRANTIES, INCLUDING, BUT NOT LIMITED TO, THE IM-PLIED WARRANTIES OF MERCHANTABILITY AND FITNESS FOR A PAR-TICULAR PURPOSE ARE DISCLAIMED. IN NO EVENT SHALL THE AUTHOR OR CONTRIBUTORS BE LIABLE FOR ANY DIRECT, INDIRECT, INCIDEN-TAL, SPECIAL, EXEMPLARY, OR CONSEQUENTIAL DAMAGES (INCLUDING, BUT NOT LIMITED TO, PROCUREMENT OF SUBSTITUTE GOODS OR SER-VICES; LOSS OF USE, DATA, OR PROFITS; OR BUSINESS INTERRUPTION) HOWEVER CAUSED AND ON ANY THEORY OF LIABILITY, WHETHER IN CONTRACT, STRICT LIABILITY, OR TORT (INCLUDING NEGLIGENCE OR OTHERWISE) ARISING IN ANY WAY OUT OF THE USE OF THIS SOFTWARE, EVEN IF ADVISED OF THE POSSIBILITY OF SUCH DAMAGE.

The licence and distribution terms for any publically available version or derivative of this code cannot be changed. i.e. this code cannot simply be copied and put under another distribution licence [including the GNU Public Licence.]

B.3.14. expat

The pyexpat extension is built using an included copy of the expat sources unless the build is configured --with-system-expat:

B.3.15. libffi

The _ctypes extension is built using an included copy of the libffi sources unless the build is configured --with-system-libffi:

B.3.16. zlib

The zlib extension is built using an included copy of the zlib sources unless the zlib version found on the system is too old to be used for the build:

2. Altered source versions must be plainly marked as such, and must not be misrepresented as being the original software.

3. This notice may not be removed or altered from any source distribution.

Jean-loup Gailly   Mark Adler

jloup@gzip.org   madler@alumni.caltech.edu

C. Copyright

Python and this documentation is:

Copyright © 2001-2011 Python Software Foundation. All rights reserved.

Copyright © 2000 BeOpen.com. All rights reserved.

Copyright © 1995-2000 Corporation for National Research Initiatives. All rights reserved.

Copyright © 1991-1995 Stichting Mathematisch Centrum. All rights reserved.

See *History and License* (page 109) for complete license and permissions information.

Other books from the publisher

Network Theory publishes books about free software under free documentation licenses. Our current catalogue includes the following titles:

- **An Introduction to Python** by Guido van Rossum and Fred L. Drake, Jr. (ISBN 978-1-906966-13-3) $19.95 (£12.95)

  This tutorial provides an introduction to Python, an easy to learn object oriented programming language. This is a revised edition for Python 3. For each copy of this manual sold, $1 is donated to the Python Software Foundation.

- **The Apache HTTP Server Reference Manual** (ISBN 978-1-906966-02-7) $29.95 (£19.95)

  This manual is a printed edition of the official Apache reference documentation from the Apache 2.2.17 distribution. It documents all the modules and configuration directives in the standard Apache 2 distribution. It also includes extensive how-to guides for mod_rewrite, virtual hosting, authentication, security, and many other topics. For each copy of this manual sold, $1 is donated to The Apache Foundation.

- **The Perl Language Reference Manual** Larry Wall et al. (ISBN 978-1-906966-02-7) $39.95 (£19.95)

  This manual is a printed edition of the official Perl reference documentation from the Perl 5.12.1 distribution. It describes the syntax of Perl and its built-in datatypes, operators, functions, variables, regular expressions and diagnostic messages. For each copy of this manual sold, $1 is donated to The Perl Foundation.

- **PostgreSQL Reference Manual: Volumes 1A, 1B, 2, 3** (ISBN 978-1-906966-04-1) $19.95 (£14.95), (ISBN 978-1-906966-05-8) $19.95 (£14.95), (ISBN 978-1-906966-06-5) $19.95 (£14.95), (ISBN 978-1-906966-07-2) $14.95 (£9.95)

  These manuals document the SQL language and commands of PostgreSQL 9.0, its client and server programming interfaces, and the configuration and maintenance of PostgreSQL servers. For each copy of these manuals sold, $1 is donated to the PostgreSQL project.

- **The Org Mode 7 Reference Manual** Carsten Dominik (ISBN: 978-1-906966-08-9) $14.95 (£9.95)

  This manual is a printed edition of the official Org reference documentation from the Org 7.3 distribution. Org mode is a powerful system for organizing projects, tasks and notes in the Emacs editor. For each copy of this manual sold, $1 is donated to the Org Project.

- **The XML 1.0 Standard (5th Edition)** W3C XML Working Group (ISBN 0954612094) $12.95 (£8.95)

  This manual is a printed edition of the Extensible Markup Language (XML) 1.0 standard from the World Wide Web Consortium. It also includes the Namespaces in XML 1.0 specification (Third Edition) and XML Information Set (Second Edition).

- **XML Path Language (XPath) 2.0 Standard** W3C XML Query and XSL Working Groups (ISBN 978-1-906966-01-0) $12.95 (£8.95)

  This manual is a printed edition of the XPath 2.0 standard from the World Wide Web Consortium.

- **GNU Bash Reference Manual** by Chet Ramey and Brian Fox (ISBN 0-9541617-7-7) $29.95 (£19.95)

  This manual is the definitive reference for GNU Bash, the standard GNU command-line interpreter. GNU Bash is a complete implementation of the POSIX.2 Bourne shell specification, with additional features from the C-shell and Korn shell. For each copy of this manual sold, $1 is donated to the Free Software Foundation.

- **An Introduction to GCC** by Brian J. Gough, foreword by Richard M. Stallman. (ISBN 0-9541617-9-3) $19.95 (£12.95)

  This manual provides a tutorial introduction to the GNU C and C++ compilers, gcc and g++. Many books teach the C and C++ languages, but this book explains how to use the compiler itself. Based on years of observation of questions posted on mailing lists, it guides the reader straight to the important options of GCC.

- **Valgrind 3.3** by J. Seward, N. Nethercote, J. Weidendorfer et al. (ISBN 0-9546120-5-1) $19.95 (£12.95)

  This manual describes how to use Valgrind, an award-winning suite of tools for debugging and profiling GNU/Linux programs. Valgrind detects memory and threading bugs automatically, avoiding hours of frustrating bug-hunting and making programs more stable. For each copy of this manual sold, $1 is donated to the Valgrind developers.

- **Comparing and Merging Files with GNU diff and patch** by David MacKenzie, Paul Eggert, and Richard Stallman (ISBN 0-9541617-5-0) $19.95 (£12.95)

  This manual describes how to compare and merge files using GNU diff and patch. It includes an extensive tutorial that guides the reader through all the options of the diff and patch commands. For each copy of this manual sold, $1 is donated to the Free Software Foundation.

- **An Introduction to R** by W.N. Venables, D.M. Smith and the R Development Core Team (ISBN 0-9541617-4-2) $19.95 (£12.95)

  This tutorial manual provides a comprehensive introduction to GNU R, a free software package for statistical computing and graphics.

- **GNU Scientific Library Reference Manual—Third Edition** by M. Galassi, et al (ISBN 0-9546120-7-8) $39.95 (£24.95)

  This reference manual is the definitive guide to the GNU Scientific Library (GSL), a numerical library for C and C++ programmers. The manual documents over 1,000 mathematical routines needed for solving problems in science and engineering. All the money raised from the sale of this book supports the development of the GNU Scientific Library.

- **GNU Octave Manual Version 3** by John W. Eaton et al. (ISBN 0-9546120-6-X) $39.95 (£24.95)

  This manual is the definitive guide to GNU Octave, an interactive environment for numerical computation with matrices and vectors. This edition covers version 3 of GNU Octave. For each copy sold $1 is donated to the GNU Octave Development Fund.

All titles are available for order from bookstores worldwide. Sales of the manuals fund the development of more free software and documentation.

For details, visit the website http://www.network-theory.co.uk/. For questions or comments, please contact sales@network-theory.co.uk.

Index

130

CPSIA information can be obtained
at www.ICGtesting.com
Printed in the USA
BVHW01s1420121217
502601BV00001B/73/P

9 781906 966140